DISTRESSED US INDUSTRIES IN THE ERA OF GLOBALIZATION

To my wife Noreena,
to my children Devi, Shanti, Hari, and Rani;
and to my grandchildren Soham and Lakshmi

-L. R.

Dedicated to the memory of my sister, Esther;
to the memory of my parents, Henoch and Sara
to my children Naomi and Avi and
their spouses Marc and Tova;
to my grandchildren
Elki, Batya, Chanoch, Devorah, Ephraim, Ayala, and Jacob;
And to my wife, Miriam;

And to that Righteous Austrian-German Officer who took my immediate
family to a hiding place just days before the last transport to Auschwitz,
where most of my family perished

-M. S.

DISTRESSED US INDUSTRIES IN THE ERA OF GLOBALIZATION

LALL RAMRATTAN

and

MICHAEL SZENBERG

ASHGATE

Published by
Ashgate Publishing Limited
Gower House
Croft Road
Aldershot
Hampshire GU11 3HR
England

Ashgate Publishing Company
Suite 420
101 Cherry Street
Burlington, VT 05401-4405
USA

Ashgate website: http://www.ashgate.com

British Library Cataloguing in Publication Data
Ramrattan, Lall, 1951-
   Distressed US industries in the era of globalization
   1. Manufacturing industries - United States
   2. Globalization - Economic aspects - United States
   3. United States - Economic conditions - 1981-2001
   4. United States - Economic conditions - 2001-
   I. Title II. Szenberg, Michael
   338.4'767'0973

   ISBN-13: 9780754670520

Library of Congress Cataloging-in-Publication Data
Ramrattan, Lall, 1951-
   Distressed US industries in the era of globalization / by Lall Ramrattan and Michael Szenberg.
         p. cm.
   Includes index.
   ISBN-13: 978-0-7546-7052-0 (alk. paper)
   1. Industries--United States. 2. Globalization--Economic aspects--United States.
   3. United States--Economic conditions--2001-
   I. Szenberg, Michael. II. Title.
   HD2785.R36 2007
   338.0973--dc22
                                                                    2007002936
ISBN 978-0-7546-7052-0

Printed and bound in Great Britain by MPG Books Ltd, Bodmin, Cornwall

Contents

List of Figures and Tables

Figures

Tables

Preface and Acknowledgments

This book presents analyses of several distressed industries in the United States, including the steel, footwear, textile and apparel, paper and publishing, and automobile industries. We particularly focus on the influence of the new era of globalization on these industries, as we argue that the transitions to their current distressed state were triggered by the structural changes that resulted from globalization. While the inevitability of the negative impact of globalization may lead some to neglect research of distressed industries, these industries continue to survive and productively contribute to the economic base of the United States. Their stories are about the changing structure, conduct, and performance of industrial United States.

Books are rarely written by single individuals. They are largely a collective undertaking since they involve interactions with many individuals. Lall and I started to work on this book sometime ago, after publishing two articles on the footwear and garment industries. The task was both intriguing and challenging at the same time. We met several years ago over the phone, while having a lengthy conversation. At that time, we formed our intellectual partnership that has been central to our work ever since. Ours is a collaborative effort par excellence.

An immense gratitude goes to P. Viswanath, a treasured and energetic colleague in the department who never tires of assisting others when asked. He accomplishes his mission with remarkable, humbling skill.

Marina Slavina, a devoted graduate assistant deserves special thanks for her ever cheerful mood and patience with the many revisions during the last year. The Finance Department's student aids Margarita Lemberg and Aparna Vasudevan have assisted us enthusiastically with this project. Our deep gratitude for their generosity.

We are grateful to Diana Ward, the Assistant Director of the Lubin's Center for Applied Research, for being most helpful and encouraging in our research efforts and to Carmen Urma, the Coordinator of Lubin's Finance and Economics Department, for lightening the department's administrative burden with aplomb. They do it with remarkable devotion and efficiency. Kudos to them.

The Pace's library is a superbly run unit where efficiency and kindness dwell together. I am grateful to the librarians of Pace University—Adele Artola, Elizabeth Birnbaum, Amerne Denton, Michelle Fanelli, Alicia Joseph and Sanda Petre, who are unfailingly enthusiastic and extraordinarily supportive.

Deep gratitude and thanks are owed to the members of the Executive Board of Omicron Delta Epsilon and the Honor Society in Economics for being an important source of support: Professors Mary Ellen Benedict, Kristine L. Chase,

James Bradley, Robert R. Ebert, William D. Gunther, Robert S. Rycroft, Kathryn A. Nantz, Farhang Niroomand and Charles F. Phillips, Jr.

And I thank my MBA and doctoral students who have sustained me for decades in this and all my work. They are really the dessert of my life.

Turning to the publishing end the book we wish to thank Brendan George, Senior Commissioning Editor at Ashgate and Carolyn Court, Editorial Administrator Social Science, who provided useful advice and support at various stages of the production. We thank the referees for the generous gift of their time. They all deserve our deepest thanks.

We thank the *International Trade Journal*, *Global Business and Economics Review*, and the *American Economist* for permission to reproduce our articles with changes. Copyright 2002 from "Trade Adjustment Assistance and Import Competition: Experience in the US Footwear Industry: 1980–1997," *International Trade Journal*, Vol. 16, No. 1, by Lall Ramrattan and Michael Szenberg. Reproduced by permission of Taylor & Francis Group, LLC., http://www. taylorandfrancis.com. Copyright 2002 from "The Post NAFTA Influence of Trade Adjustment Assistance on the US Garment Industry," *Global Business and Economics Review* (*GBER*), Vol. 4, No. 1. Granted by the *GBER* editor, Demetri Kantarelis, http://www.besiweb.com.

And now welcome to the world of the distressed US industries.

Chapter 1

Introduction

The New Era of Globalization

This book investigates the influence of the new era of globalization on several distressed United States industries. Globalization has unleashed the forces of capitalism across the world, providing United States industries with both the opportunity to produce for global consumption and to compete internationally. As was inevitable, some United States industries prospered and others struggled; some countries surged and others were unsuccessful. Japan thrived in the 1980s; Germany was a role model before unification; and the Asian Tigers thrived, only to be challenged by the 1997 Asian crisis. Within the dynamics of success and failure, new policy actions and reactions emerged. Most notably, a number of major regions integrated, resulting in structures such as NAFTA and the European Union. The General Agreement on Tariffs and Trade (GATT), formed in 1947, became the World Trade Organization (WTO) in 1995. Liberalization of trade dissolved impediments, and as countries and governments became more efficient, tariffs and quotas decreased from approximately 40 per cent to 4 per cent. Profit potential for industries increased and welfare gains for countries were realized.

The intense wave of globalization from 1980 to the present has brought benefits to many private citizens, governments, firms, industries, and countries. One perspective is that these gains resulted from the forces of free trade and liberalization. Another perspective is that these gains resulted from improvements in the factors of production such as land, labor, capital, technical progress, and the now fashionable term "human capital" that includes human ability and effort. A third perspective is that these gains resulted from changes in the social, political, and cultural environments.

Depending on how industries adapted to these changes, the intense wave of globalization led to benefits or costs. In this book, we examine how the positive forces of globalization have influenced several distressed industries. Production requires capital. Therefore, we first examine the role that capital plays in growth and productivity. John Maynard Keynes tells us that capital accumulation in Britain began when Sir Francis Drake made off with a hefty loot from a Spanish fleet coming from Peru in 1580 (Keynes 1963, 362), and the growth that followed was based on the magic of compound interest. Looting is no longer necessary, at least not the type of looting Sir Francis Drake practiced. Instead, capital has become more mobile across borders than labor. The term "competition" has lost some of its primacy in the era of globalization, as governments subsidize exports and provide protection from imports. As citizens complain about foreign firms making monopoly profits, governments step in to collect some of the monopoly rents through taxes, tariffs, voluntary agreements, quotas, and the like.

In the era of globalization, some industries gain as bystanders from spillover growth, some gain from government subsidies and protection, and some suffer. Two types of equilibria influence these results: optimal tariff equilibrium and free trade equilibrium. If global trade cannot operate without protection, then there is a level of tariff that yields the highest or optimal gains. Strategic trade theory argues that a government can use tariffs as a strategy in a game with other countries to help a domestic firm or industry gain from trade. Consider a foreign firm that has some monopoly power when trading with a country; the government can justify intervention on a firm's or industry's behalf. It is a natural tendency for trading blocks, Free Trade Agreements (FTA), and larger countries to attempt to exercise market power. They may wish to restrict exports in order to influence world prices. The formation of the European Union can be perceived as an attempt by Europe to create parity with North America, as a reaction to NAFTA. From this perspective, trading blocks act as stumbling blocks to free trade on the hypothesis that countries that form FTAs, such as NAFTA and the EU, tend to reduce tariffs among themselves and increase tariffs against nonmember countries, working against free trade. Some may argue that optimal tariffs are a step towards free trade. However, optimal tariffs give greater gains to some countries that would rather not turn to free trade under those circumstances.

In line with modern research, we may argue that movement away from tariffs towards freer trade is a superior policy. To examine this argument we need to consider the concept of efficiency. Essentially, free trade competition establishes Pareto optimal outcomes through the first welfare theorem in welfare economics, whereas under optimal tariff equilibrium, such an efficient condition does not hold. In practice, what we experience is not a Pareto optimal outcome under the first welfare theorem, but an inefficient outcome under the second welfare theorem. To illustrate, the movement from optimal tariff to free trade equilibrium in a closed economy (autarky) requires the redistribution of gains from one agent to another, and movement in the open economy requires a mechanism that redistributes benefits from one country to another in order to maintain efficiency. Consider movement from autarky to free trade. Assume that one factor, labor, gains from free trade, while another factor, capital, is not worse off. The factor that gains from trade can potentially compensate the other factor that loses, thereby improving welfare benefits. The bottom line is that mutual gain from trade is not assured, i.e., "it is not necessarily true that both would gain from the restoration of world free trade—to establish free trade to mutual benefit, it may be necessary for one country to offer an income transfer to another" (Krauss and Johnson 1974, 174 and 242). However, such potential gains can materialize indirectly. Kyle Bagwell and Robert W. Staiger (2002, xii), for instance, argue that a country might bargain with another in order to access its market in exchange for a lower terms-of-trade concession, such as a lower tariff rate. Under short-run temporary Walrasian equilibrium, a country, regardless of size, can attain competitive equilibrium with a "sagacious" redistribution schema. Under some technical assumptions, gains from trade are a proven outcome (Grandmont and McFadden 1972, 110–14).

The traditional literature focuses on the zero sum gains among countries as they move through a sequence of regimes that converge in free trade. In the modern literature this sequence moves typically from autarky to optimal tariffs to various trade zones, and ultimately to free trade. As countries play their best strategies in games where action-reaction patterns such as tariff wars can result, both zero-sum and other outcomes associated with the "prisoner's dilemma" scenario can arise. Such results were noted in a subset of distressed industries where "(t)he textile, apparel, and footwear industries in the rich industrial nations have all been hit hard by competition from the newly industrializing countries ... Protection against imports has been the only important policy adopted to help American firms in these industries adjust to changing market conditions" (Aggarwal and Haggard 1983, 249).

A Set of Distressed United States Industries

Why are some industries distressed in the presence of free trade and liberalization? The steel industry is distressed because it was slow to adopt the new and more efficient technology which its competitor, Nucor, has pioneered for global competition. The footwear industry is distressed because the technology it uses is easy to imitate by foreign producers. The pharmaceutical industry is distressed because it is difficult to develop a new chemical element (NCE) that is safe and that passes the Federal Drug Administration's (FDA) rigorous standards. It takes 12 to 15 years and many parallel researchers attempt to come up with an NCE, while competitors can develop generic drugs in a much shorter time. Therefore, the pharmaceutical industry requires longer patent protection and the ability to enforce licenses abroad in order to recoup its research and development costs.

One reason why the garment industry is distressed is that the jobs they offer are at the low end of the manufacturing wage scale (Hufbauer and Schott 1992, 266). According to the United States International Trade Commission (USITC), developed countries have lost over half of their productive capacity in the apparel industry to less developed countries over the last three decades (USITC 1995, 1). The effects of technology on global competition can be demonstrated by the statement that "a garment could be designed in New York, produced from a fabric made in Australia, spread and cut in Hong Kong, assembled in China, and eventually distributed in Germany" (Mittelhauser 1997, 25).

The paper and publishing industry is in trouble in the new global market because Internet technology has broken the monopoly that local bookstores, for instance, used to enjoy (Brynjolfsson 2001, 106). Local monopoly prices are no longer possible with competitors such as Amazon.com. "Vast unquantifiable spillover benefits accrue to users of published materials in the form of education, transfer of technology, advances in science and industry, the creation of new types of employment, and improvement in social services and indeed in the overall economic growth of countries" (United Nations 2002, 159).

The United States auto industry is in trouble because "giantism and high market concentration have failed to promote innovation and technological advances in the field" (Adams and Brock 2004, 48). The auto industry did not plan in a timely way the innovation of fuel efficient cars, and during the repeated rounds of oil price increases engineered by the OPEC starting in the 1970s foreign firms were able to make significant inroads into domestic firms' market shares (ibid., 68).

The new economy, dominated by information technology for productivity and growth, has not rendered these distressed industries unproductive, redundant, or useless. A brief look at the productivity data indicates that from 1994 to 2000 the electronic and electrical industries were leaders, contributing approximately 2.5 per cent to productivity. The industrial machinery sector, the next largest contributor, added about 1.75 per cent to productivity. All the other industries were far below the third contributor, the chemicals and allied product industry, which contributed approximately 0.75 percentage points. Other industries with positive productivity growth were in the range of approximately 0.02 percentage points. The distressed industries live within the range of productivity growth that engulfs most of the other industries with low growth. Primary and fabricated metals, textile and apparel products, leather, and rubber are led by motor vehicles in the low productivity range. While the printing and publishing sector indicates a negative percentage, when merged with paper and allied products it indicates, at worst, a flat growth rate (Nordhaus 2002, 235). It appears, therefore, that the growing IT sector is accompanied by distressed industries at the lower end of the economic base.

This is not an altogether bad position for a government to take because it can use the tariff revenues to provide public goods if the demand for those goods exists. As a rule, United States industries seek protection from competitive products that can be produced in low wage countries, as well as subsidies for agricultural products (Weintraub 2004, 2). For example, one of the impediments to the FTA agreement is that the United States does not want to drop its protection of the concentrated orange juice industry from Brazilian competitors. On the other hand, while foreign countries are known to seek protection for their "infant" industries, they are much more concerned as to whether gains from trade will benefit the majority of their citizens. Critical institution of trade must be established to allocate efficiently resources such as labor, capital, and technology, and such institutions may invariably require some level of protection. It is worth stating that even Adam Smith made exceptions to the rule of free trade by allowing some protection when a rival country puts a duty on its goods and services: "The case in which it may sometimes be a matter of deliberation how far it is proper to continue the free importation of certain foreign goods, is, when some foreign nation restrains by high duties or prohibitions the importation of some of our manufactures into their country" (Smith 1976, 467).

The current practice among distressed industries is to seek protection in the form of tariffs, quotas, restraints, or restriction of licenses. According to the International Trade Commission (ITC), the United States' import of textiles and apparel made up 24 per cent of world imports by value in 2002, and are "subject to quota restrictions and to tariff rates that are among the highest of any product sector" (USITC 2004, 59). For the footwear industry, the tariff rate on rubber and plastic imports was approximately 11.8 per cent in 2002. The steel industry was able to convince a free trade president, George W. Bush, to increase tariffs and tariff-rate quotas on 14 categories of steel output in March 2002. Voluntary restraints (1969–1974), minimum price arrangement (1978–1982), import quotas (1982–1992), and a battery of temporary restrictions on the steel industry that were removed by President Bush in March 2003 and 2004 are some of the major protectors of the steel industry. In the pharmaceutical industry, the reluctance of United States firms to license their products abroad represents a stumbling block for freer trade (Hufbauer and Schott 1992, 179). For the publishing industry, copyright protection has established property rights, a prerequisite for gains from trade. The International Intellectual Property Alliance (IIPA) estimates that annual losses due to piracy of copyrighted United States material are in the range of $20–22 billion annually (UN 2002, 172–3). "The 1981 voluntary export restraint agreement with Japan on automobiles marked the first overt attempt to protect the U.S. automobile industry from imports since World War II" (Crandall 1987, 271).

The traditional benefits provided for distressed industries include relatively high paying jobs, consumer or producer benefits (surpluses), and the resulting tax (tariff) revenues for the government. Without these benefits, Bagwell and Staiger's (2000) arguments for consumer benefits and tariffs to enhance GATT/ WTO liberalization efforts would not stand. In the long run, survival will depend on the net benefits; in such a time frame, we expect Adam Smith's maxim to apply: "It is the maxim of every prudent master of a family, never to attempt to make at home what it will cost him more to make than to buy" (Smith 1976, 456). For example, when Bethlehem Steel filed for bankruptcy in October 15, 2001, no one thought it had a sufficiently strong business model to survive; in particular, markets looked askance at its approximately 14,000 employees, and the five times that number on its retirement roll. Another example is Burlington Industries, which allowed Polaroid to fail because its technology became obsolete with the advent of digital technology.

The state of the distressed industries is related to arguments for and against protection on the one hand, and free trade and liberalization on the other. In the modern trade literature, the favorable arguments for free trade rest on the premises of "(1) increased exploitation of economies of scale, (2) enhanced diversity of choice among differentiated goods, (3) ... x-efficiency ... pressuring firms to upgrade the productivity of their resource use instead of 'goofing off,'...

(4) the demonstrated possibility that trade can be a conduit for know-how ...,
and (5) increased marginal efficiency of capital" (Bhagwati 2002, 35–6). The
unfavorable arguments for freer trade rest on the ideas of unequal distribution
of incomes, environmental concerns, labor standards, and human rights concerns
(ibid., 44).

A narrower scope of the investigation at hand would involve studying
the distressed industries from the points of view of efficiency and the market
mechanism, equity—concerns about social justice and fairness—TAA, and
income inequality (Kapstein 2000, 373). In modern times, efficiency and policy are
dominant concerns, at least in theory. The political point of view came out clearly
during the 2004 presidential debates. President Bush emphasized the dominant
political policy position, namely, the need for educating impacted workers. He
subsequently announced an expansion of funding for the TAA program. In the
rest of this chapter, we present the free trade, protectionist, and liberalization
backgrounds for our set of distressed industries. In the next chapter, we present
the TAA/policy background information for our study.

Efficiency: Definition and Relation to Market Structure under Free Trade and Competition

The most celebrated name in the efficiency literature is Vilfredo Pareto. He
wrote:

> A consideration of the size of industrial enterprises leads us to recognize that there
> exists in general a definite *maximum* at which the expansion of enterprises stops under
> a regime of free competition, there being no advantage in increasing them beyond or
> leaving them short of what corresponds to this magnitude (Pareto 1887, 492).

In the same vein, he wrote:

> We will say that the members of a collectivity enjoy *maximum ophelimity* in a certain
> position when it is impossible to find a way of moving from that position very slightly
> in such a manner that the ophelimity enjoyed by each of the individuals of that
> collectivity increases or decreases. That is to say, any small displacement in departing
> from that position necessarily has the effect of increasing the ophelimity which certain
> individuals enjoy, and decreasing that which others enjoy, of being agreeable to some,
> and disagreeable to others (Pareto 1906, 261).

The concept of Pareto efficiency has undergone many transformations to
tailor it to the study of firms and industries. Walter Adams and James W. Brock
wrote of operations, innovations, and social efficiencies (Adams and Brock 2004,
11–76). The former is built around production at the lowest cost (ibid., 30), and
fits with the comparative cost advantage in trade theory. Innovation efficiency is
concerned with the creation of better products and production processes (ibid.,

46), and countries are taking advantage of the new information technology. Social efficiency "means producing the most desirable combination of goods and services from among those that are technologically feasible" (ibid., 63). It is concerned with consumer and producer surpluses, and is therefore directly linked to gains from trade.

Did free trade and liberalization create an inefficiency problem for distressed United States industries? We know that free trade is associated with perfect competition, which assumes a homogeneous product and ease of entry and exit. However, efficiency is often associated with the notion of competition without any theoretical basis (Schwartzman 1973, 763–4). Under the assumption of perfect competition, profit maximization implies technical efficiency because producers are inclined to select the best or most efficient technique. But there is no implication that all aspects of efficiency, such as employee morale and good levels of management, are present.

Pareto efficiency that results in gains from free trade is often associated with a compensation principle that implies some form of compensation for distressed United States industries. "There are two alternative techniques for demonstrating that a country is potentially better off with free trade than under self sufficiency, the first utilizing individual preferences functions, the second the community indifference map" (Krauss and Johnson 1974, 172). In the first case, the compensation principle for Pareto efficiency requires that the gaining factor, (e.g., labor) must compensate the harmed factor (e.g., capital) for injuries from free trade. In the second case, given an improvement in the terms of trade that affects the consumer or producer, free trade would imply a permutation of subsidies or tariffs on the consumers or the producers (ibid., 175).

On the pragmatic side, Pareto efficiency in terms of Stochastic Frontier Efficiency in a production or cost function has implications for distressed industries. To the extent that distressed industries prevent a country from being on its stochastic efficient frontier, they will affect a country's ranking in the efficient use of resources and technology. For instance, Schumpeter (1939, 87) has defined "an innovation as the setting up of a new production function." In order to rank countries' adoption of new technology, Ramrattan, DiMeglio, and Szenberg (2004) have fitted telecom data to production functions for 69 countries of the modern global economies for the 2000–2002 period. The stochastic production efficiency concept is highlighted through making Output = f(Inputs), where given Inputs, the observed Output must be less than or equal to f(Inputs) (ibid., 36). The stochastic production efficiency concept accounts for the adoption of new technology as it diffused across nations in the modern global economy. Industries that are slow to adopt new innovations and technology will fall behind and become distressed, but if they are protected, they may recover when they enhance efficiency.

Sometimes, in analyzing distressed industries, one should consider efficiency at the more disaggregated firm level, studying strategies among them. Efficiency at the firm level is built around equilibrium such as Bertrand, or Nash. Spencer and Brander (1983, 717) have argued that a government has a role in certain industries that are important to the "strategic game." Their model predicts that, as export subsidies decrease in a liberalization environment, "the government has an incentive to tax R&D to restore domestic production efficiency, and to use an export subsidy to enable domestic firms to capture a larger share of the industry than it would unaided" (ibid.,). The nature of the game is such that the "policy tool in question might be tariffs, quotas, voluntary export restraints, R&D subsidies or any one of a wide range of policy instruments" (Brander 1995, 8). In this type of game, the concept of efficiency is lost. To the extent that the firms are monopolistic, we know that price will be above marginal cost, and that equilibrium will be reached when average cost is still falling. "One important aspect of imperfect competition is that the price charged for a good exceeds the marginal cost of production ... a country has an incentive to extract rent from foreign exporters by using tariffs" (Brander and Spencer 1981, 372). However, as "imperfectly competitive goods tend to be underprovided from the overall world point of view, therefore, other things equal, policies that subsidize such goods actually tend to enhance overall efficiency" (Brander 1995, 66).

Last but not least, distressed industries can gain efficiency through consolidation, bargaining, or merging. Examples of consolidation in the steel industry include Jones & Laughlin Steel and Youngstown Sheet & Tube in 1978, and LTV and Republic Steel in 1984. More recently, US Steel and International Steel were poised to acquire the failed Bethlehem Steel in 2003. In the pharmaceutical industry, SmithKline and Beecham merged in 1989, Glaxo and Wellcome merged in 1995, and finally these two entities merged with each other in 2000. Also, Pharmacia and Upjohn merged in 1995 and Pfizer and Warner-Lambert merged in 1999. There are plans for further mergers, and many mergers in the prescription drug area. In the book industry, Barnes and Noble and Ingram Book Group had plans to merge. In the footwear industry, the old case of Brown Shoe v. United States (1962) was a trend-setter. The auto industry is also replete with mergers from the days of the independents. More recently, in 1987, Chrysler merged with American Motors because it needed the excess capacity for expansion. Also, there were "global consolidations—Ford acquiring Jaguar, Volvo, Land Rover, and Mazda; GM acquiring Saab and Fiat; the Chrysler-Daimler merger" (Adams and Brock 2004, 34–5, 164). There have also been a plethora of cross-ownerships and joint ventures.

The quest for mergers and joint ventures among distressed industries brings up the question of efficiency from the cooperative game theory point of view. Given a company's stake and endowment, what is the optimal number of collations that should be formed, and how are the benefits to be distributed? For the auto industry, GM, Ford, and Chrysler engaged in joint production, ownership stakes, joint research, and vehicle supply and distribution types of collaborations with foreign firms (Adams and Brock 1995, 75). On the splitting of gains, we can think of allocating one dollar to be divided by two firms. One may have 75 cents and the other 25. If the latter feels that it can improve its position, it would be inclined to bargain, until, say, a 50/50 split is achieved. When we get to a position where we cannot improve one firm's benefit without hurting another firm, we have reached a high level of efficiency.

Trade Models for the Analysis of Distressed Industries: Efficiency, Free Trade, Strategic Trade, and Protectionism

In this section, to generate an understanding of policy positions related to distressed industries, we summarize the theoretical foundations behind the arguments for modern gains from trade as they relate to the distressed industries. Mercantilists thrived on government-created monopoly power to conduct their foreign trade; this suggests that one country's gain requires actions that hurt other countries. Do such zero-sum scenarios exist today? To Adam Smith "every individual, it is evident, can, in his local situation, judge much better than any statesman or lawgiver can do for him" (Smith 1976, 456).

With free-trade, workers in an import-impacted industry experience lower pay and capitalists suffer a lower return on their investment. Not only individuals, but entire regions of a country may be hurt by free trade. This suggests that job losses in the United States are matched by jobs gained abroad, and that, by symmetry, wages and rates of return on investment abroad will improve. But the magic of free trade holds that United States losses may be more than offset by gains for the United States from abroad. As Samuelson notes, it "is valid to state that free trade increases worldwide efficiency" (Samuelson 1986, Volume V, 484).

One theoretical issue is the question of how to measure gains. One perspective is that free trade places traders in all industries, including distressed industries, on a world production-possibility frontier that is superior to where the trader would be placed otherwise. Free trade can also be understood using regional utility curves, though there are problems in aggregating these curves. In freer trade, potential gains can more than offset what a single player loses, though no guarantee exists that a Japan, or a China, or a United States will gain.

D. Ricardo, J.S. Mill, F.Y. Edgeworth, W. Pareto

John Stuart Mill said once of David Ricardo's model

> it is established, that the advantage which two countries derive from trading with each other, results from the more advantageous employment which thence arises, of the labour and capital—for shortness let us say the labour—or both jointly. The circumstances are such that if each country confines itself to the production of one commodity, there is a greater total return to the labour of both together; and this increase of produce forms the whole of what the two countries taken together gain by the trade (Mill 1967, 235).

Ricardo did not flesh out all the details of his models. He did not show how the gains ought to be divided between the two nations. Mill himself attempted to fill that gap, noting that

> the whole gain to both countries together, consisting in the saving of labour; and the saving of labour being exactly equal to the difference between the costs, in the two countries, of the one commodity as compared with the other; the two countries taken together gain no more than this difference; and if either country gains the whole of it, the other country derives no advantage from the trade (ibid.,).

One might argue that the cost difference is reflective of transportation expenses. Francis Edgeworth credits Henry Sedgwick for first raising the question (Edgeworth 1894, 619). He also illustrates how we can account for the parameters that cause gains and losses to trade, and isolates some difficulties it causes while distributing the pie, so to speak, following guidelines laid down by Mill. Edgeworth recognizes Alfred Marshall's simplification of the problem as a supply and demand issue (Edgeworth 1894, 424). He makes an analogy between trade and a clock. Just as the hands of a clock are driven by an internal adjustment mechanism, gains from trade are also driven by an internal mechanism. Hence, there is no need to make constant assumptions about costs and marginal utilities of imports and exports (ibid., 425–43). Instead, it is possible to get a variety of changes in supply and demand by combining positive and negative changes, though the potential number of cases can be in the hundreds (ibid., 525). As some of those changes will be more important than others, a player needs to study only the cases most important to his circumstances (Edgeworth 1894, 605, 608).

No definitive proof that a country can gain from free trade exists. We suspect, however, that there is some credence to the idea. Initially, we consider simple models, analogous to a model of the nature of heavy objects fall within a vacuum, which is then complicated by other factors, such as the resistance of air. Pareto (1897, 490) assures us that "such are the considerations which lead to the method of successive approximations in political economy." It is not the rigor of mathematics that is of interest. Rigor can be attained by good logic. What mathematics brings to the table is that "it permits us to treat problems far more complicated than those generally solved by ordinary logic" (ibid., 491). In order to appreciate further the mathematical development of trade theory (to aid our understanding of distressed industries), we should note a wise summary of the situation as follows:

> If our equations are constructed each for a homogeneous group, and several of these groups are considered, we get the theory of non-competing groups of Cairns and an effectively complete theory of international trade, together with an adequate scientific interpretation of the theory of comparative cost. By use of these general formulas we find the coefficients of production. A consideration of their variability leads us up to a recognition of the function of the entrepreneurs and to the theory of different systems of production according as we postulate either free competition or monopoly

or a socialistic regime. It is to be borne in mind that consumers are reckoning in terms of marginal utility or "ophelimity," while the entrepreneur is counting in terms of money (ibid., 492).

P.A. Samuelson and F.A. Hayek

The study of distressed industries can be further highlighted by some of Samuelson's contributions to trade theory. For him, "economic law suggests … that much of the manufacturing industry will try to leave Western Europe and North America under free trade" (Samuelson 1986, 511). "The purpose of economic theory is to alert us to the direction of change … economic theory also has the normative purpose of setting out the likely consequences of alternative policy programs." But, "the deductive syllogism that free trade maximizes each market participant's welfare is logically false. Even under strict conditions most suitable for perfect competition particular market participants win and lose from ever-occurring shifts in supply and demand." But these shifts will likely average out in the long run under free trade (ibid., 511–12).

A novel insight of Samuelson's is that "under free trade both parties are better off than under no trade at all, but are not necessarily in the optimum position" (Samuelson 1966, Volume 2, 779). Two auxiliary hypotheses come out of this:

1. The essence of trade is gain. All agents can abstain from trade, but engage in trade as trade improves their conditions.

2. The results under conditions of perfect competition are not the optimal outcomes. Why? In an extreme case, equilibrium is obtained when one country gains all and the other gains nothing, or at best only "an infinitesimal gain from trade," perhaps because of haggling in the marketplace. Samuelson argues "nothing said here is in fundamental contradiction to the orthodox theory of comparative cost in international trade… Furthermore, this thesis must not be construed as being necessarily contrary to the political question of free (or freer) trade … But … it would seem desirable to clarify economic theory on these issues" (ibid., 780).

Samuelson's theorem adds a perspective through which to analyze distressed industries. For example, consider the results of the equalization of factor prices, and that the increase in relative prices of a good increases demand for the factors to make those goods, thereby increasing the returns to those factors, and lowering the returns to factors that produce other goods, according to Stolper and Samuelson (1941). Broadly speaking, under a situation of two factors and two or more goods, we can fathom results that make general predictions for trade such as:

1) winner or loser where free trade is not good for everyone;
2) factor-industry detachment where external price changes affect factor return regardless of the industry involved;
3) scarce-factor is helped by protection while abundant factor is hurt;

4) a factor that has enough of a scarcity will not be hurt; and
5) price-signal response where an external shock is communicated to price, and not via quantity.

These points make for a Samuelsonian paradigm in trade theory. To further build the intuition of productivity of free trade, Friedrich Hayek gave an illustration where the production of a commodity in one part of the world may depend on a small quantity of another commodity that is available in another remote part of the world (Hayek 1988, 94). But he adds, "The idea that such productivity, and even such bringing together of supplies, also depends on a continuous successful search for widely dispersed and constantly changing information remains harder to grasp" (ibid., 94), and "trade ... brought not only individual but also collective wealth through effort of brain rather than of muscles" (ibid., 93).

Strategic Trade Theory

Over the past 50 years, gains from trade, which seem to have no parallel in history, are attributed to policy measures that moved the economy toward free trade and away from protectionism.[1] Liberalization leads to gains from trade because it yields (Dornbusch 1993, 87):

1) better allocation of resources;
2) better technology;
3) economies of scale and scope;
4) greater competition at home;
5) improved externality conditions;
6) transfer of know-how; and
7) better opportunities for some industries to achieve growth.

Trade theory since World War II has the unique characteristic of being built on the concept of market imperfections or distortions. For example, Hayek showed that trade occurs because countries complement each other. Trading was facilitated by technological developments in transportation, such as railroads and steamships, and communication developments, such as the transatlantic telegraph. Strategic trade is more substitutional, involving advanced nations "taking in each other's

---

[1]   According to Anne O. Krueger (2003, 21–2), "Rapidly falling transport and communications costs have helped, of course. But the dismantling of trade barriers that took place after 1945 fuelled economic growth. The multilateral trade system set up first under the GATT (General Agreement of Tariffs and Trade) and now overseen by the World Trade Organization helped all participating countries reap the benefits of free, or freer, trade. We must not lose sight of the role that trade liberalization has played in creating the gains in economic welfare from which so many people have benefited."

washing," so to speak (Krugman 1994, 231). To be fair, Mill predicted this type of trading long ago, writing that "it is probable that our trade with the colonies, and with the countries which send us the raw materials of our international industry, is not more but less advantageous to us, in proportion to its extent, than our trade with the continent of Europe. We mean in respect to the mere amount of the return to the labor and capital of the country; considered abstractedly from the usefulness or agreeableness of the particular articles on which the receivers may choose to expend it" (Mill 1967, 261). Krugman (1994a, 231) argued that this type of trading explains the fact that advanced countries have increased their exports from 38 per cent in 1953 to 76 per cent in 1990.

While Krugman's predictions coincide with Mill's, his reasons are more modern. Nations trade because:

1) Skill and knowledge give the United States an advantage in the production of aircraft and much of new trade is in this form of commodities,
2) Governments support the international competition of their home firms,
3) A country behaves as though it no longer has monopolistic power in the face of foreign competition, but now identifies with "sunrise" or "high-value" industries, and
4) "The ideas of strategic traders seemed to the economists to be a set of crude misconceptions, presented as if they were sophisticated insights" (ibid., 232–256).

One misconception is that trade follows the law of competition, when in reality it depends on performance (ibid., 287). Fixation on competitiveness by the strategic trade theorist has negative consequences; it leads to trade wars and invites protectionism. This emphasizes the external aspect of trade. Another misconception of strategic trade theory is that it overemphasizes the international over the internal issues such as budget, health care, and environment (ibid., 290).

Strategic trade confronts arguments that trading under imperfect market conditions (distortions or market failures), such as sticky wages, may give occasion for free trade to impact economic welfare negatively (Haberler 1950). This argument is against free trade, as pointed out by Jagdish Bhagwati in an interview with Balasubramanyam (www.columbia.edu/~jb38/index_profiles. html), Gottfried Haberler was the first to criticize free trade. Keynes has given us the ideas of imperfect market conditions such as interest inelasticity, liquidity trap, and wage rigidity. Joan Robinson and Edward Chamberlin established that imperfect markets arise from monopoly and competition, elements that introduce inefficiency into trading. As summarized by Hicks (1959, 46), "if apparent costs only equal true costs under conditions of perfect competition and competition is hardly ever perfect, the bottom seems to drop out of the Free Trade argument." Perhaps for the reason that Hicks gave, the free trade paradigm degenerated after World War II.

In the 1960s, Bhagwati saw a way to make the degenerating free trade paradigm more progressive. His idea was to work within the domain of Samuelson's paradigm to justify the proposition that some trade is better than no trade (Bhagwati et al., 1998, 265). In order to understand this proposition, we should take a detour through the Heckscher-Ohlin (HO) theory. In modern HO trade theory under perfect markets, increased efficiency either increases output from an improved allocation of labor and capital, or reduces the cost of a factor by reducing labor and/or capital requirements. The net effect is a shift in the community's production possibility curve (PPC) (Kenen 1994, 127). A country's PPC can shift to reflect changes in capital and/or labor. The famous Rybczynski theorem states that, if increased factors are fully employed, and factor requirements are given, then an increase in the supply of one factor of production raises the output of the good that uses that factor intensively and reduces the output of the other goods (Kenen 1994, 70).

Three concepts of optimum in economic operations are useful to assess efficiency. First, the Marginal Rate of Substitution (MRS) by individuals among goods must equal the ratio of marginal utilities from that good, which is the standard equilibrium condition for consumer equilibrium.. Second, the factors of production must be utilized such that the Marginal Rate of Technical Substitution (MRTS) among factors must equal the factors' marginal product. Third, optimal production is attained where the Marginal Rate of Transformation (MRT) between goods must equal the MRS. Where MRT ≠ MRS, we would increase production of low cost goods, and decrease the production of high cost goods. The result is that a person will be able to attain a higher indifference curve without worsening the conditions of another individual (Herbener 1997, 86).

To analyze the welfare of a nation, we need social or welfare indifference and production possibilities curves. Abram Bergson (1982, 2–27, 154) was the first to actually write out such a mathematical welfare function: $W = F(U^1, U^2, U^3 \dots .)$ and has shown that it is a "generalization of the Marshall-Pigou formulation; according to the latter, W is the sum of the utilities U^1, U^2, U^3, and so on. Also, to maximize W would satisfy the criterion of Pareto and Barone." But for the Samuelson-Bergson utility function, the rapid stride of Computational General Equilibrium analysis would have been dealt a severe blow. In explaining their GTAP model that allows the calculation of welfare gains from trade in the modern global economy, Thomas Hertel and Marinos Tsigas (1998, 15) wrote that "the greatest advantage of the formulation of regional expenditure … is the unambiguous indicator of welfare offered by the regional utility function."

A social or national PPC can be derived from individual PPCs as follows. First, bring in the international price ratio tangent to the PPC. Second, make it tangent to a utility curve in the northwest direction above the PPC curve, staying in the positive quadrant. Third, create a triangle with the two tangent points, and a third point in the PPC region. The base of a triangle so formed will measure the country's export; its height, the country's import. One observation is that trade is beneficial for the autarky country, which by entering into trade is able to move beyond its PPC. The benefits are driven by the country's ability to trade at a lower price and by a more efficient use of resources that follows from remixing autarky resources to produce for export. Another observation is that the rest of the world (ROW) must have a mirror image of this triangle. It must be willing to export a magnitude measured by the vertical segment, and import the magnitude indicated by the horizontal segment of the triangle.

As summarized by Bhagwati et al. (1998, 271) we now have two theorems:

- A Technology Theorem, where the production possibility curve (PPC) is covered by a Baldwin Envelope Curve (BEC, a straight line for a small country), where every point on the PPC curve Pareto dominates every point on the BEC curve so that "one can have more of one good and no less of the other for every vector of autarkic output" (Bhagwati et al. 1998, 265).
- A Utility Theorem: If we derive an autarky utility possibility curve for the PPC curve, and a trade utility curve from the BEC curve, then we reach the same conclusion as in theorem one that "the utility-possibility locus in the trade situation will Pareto-dominate the utility-possibility locus in the autarkic situation" (Bhagwati et al. 1998, 267).

Theorems 1 and 2 show that "Free trade is optimal for a competitive small economy" (Bhagwati et al. 1998, 271). But we cannot kill two birds with one stone; instead we need one policy for the attainment of free trade, and one for distortions (market failure). This free trade proposition requires the use of the Lagrangian maximization function:

$$\Phi = Y - \lambda_1[Q_1 - \varphi(Q_2)] - \lambda_2[E_1 - \psi(M_2)] - \lambda_3[C_1 - Q_1 - E_1] - \lambda_4[C_2 - Q_2 - M_2]$$

where: $U = U(C_1, C_2)$ is the utility function, and the constraints are

1 $Q_1 = \varphi(Q_2)$

2 $E_1 = \psi(M_2)$

3 $C_1 = Q_1 - E_1$

4 $C_2 = Q_2 - M_2$

where Q is output, E is export, M is import, and C is consumption (Bhagwati et al. 1998, 271–3). The first order conditions for maximum, which do not look for turning points, is that the Domestic Rate of Transformation (DRT) = Foreign Rate of Substitution (FRT) =Domestic rate of Substitution (DRS).

Free trade will lead to many optimal solutions. One has to recall Joan Robinson's dictum that "… the theory of Value and Distribution does not depict a single system of prices; it consists of a variety of systems, each appropriate to the model of a different kind of economy" (Robinson 1962, 1). In fact, the first order condition shows an infinite number of such Pareto-optimal world-welfare solutions.

We next consider the various permutations of imperfect markets in the picture. The literature is already extensive on this matter. The essence of the model is that it is possible to get equilibrium conditions that are not efficient. This is a natural prediction of monopolistic competition models that, for instance, indicate that p > mc, incurring deadweight losses to society and production with excess capacity. Strategic trade theory shows that the government has an important role to play in such trading situations. It can subsidize its high-value industries through export strategies or impose quotas or tariffs on imports of foreign competitive products. Such governmental policy will incur cost to the domestic consumers, but will enable benefits to the producers and, depending on the permutation of subsidies or tariffs, the next result of welfare benefits to the country would be gains to trade. A survey by James Brander (1995, 1438) in *The Handbook of International Economics* shows how strategic trade models under game theory are calibrated for several industries, including the auto industry. Another survey by Robert Feenstra (1989) demonstrates variation on the estimates of one of the techniques that can be used for application to other industries.

What we have assessed in the trade literature so far is that the gains-from-trade arguments give credence to continued efforts toward free trade as a goal. We stand by the point that the distressed industries may not able to ride the wave of more favorable free trade in the modern global economy. Other arguments against trade that are sociological or political in nature exist as well. For instance, "trade may have some adverse impact on wage inequality" (Kapstein 2000, 360). The often-cited Bureau of Census data indicates that the bottom fifth percentile of families' share of the before-tax income decreased from 5.2 per cent in 1980 to 4.6 per cent in 1990, and 4.3 per cent in 2000. At the same time, the top fifth percentile's share increased by 15.3, 17.4, and 20.8 per cent, respectively. A major textbook by Mankiw explains that technology and trade with low income countries have reduced demand for unskilled labor, and raised the demand for skilled labor, causing the relative wages of low income workers to fall (Mankiw 2004, 431). Others disagree: "Trade liberalization is neither the primary motor of U.S. corporate growth nor the basis of today's global economy ... administration committed to trade liberalization made it necessary for these trade-sensitive industries to restructure—to change the way they organized their production and sales, to respond to a new, more wage-competitive environment" (Rosen 2002, 6–7).

Efficiency and Growth

The Doha Round of trade negotiations was premised on the argument that liberalization will help developing countries grow approximately 5.5 per cent after

10 to 20 years, and reduce poverty by 20 per cent (Cline 2004). On the other hand, the Bush administration granted the steel industry temporary tariff protection to allow it to grow. This tariff protection was granted with full knowledge of a controversy in the granting of an earlier protection to this industry for tinplates through the controversial McKinley tariff of the 1930s. The argument was that United States prices of iron and steel were approaching those of the United Kingdom, and therefore protection was unnecessary and costly (Irwin 2000). Do both liberalization and protection then allow industries to grow? Modern "endogenous," as opposed to the old "exogenous," theories help to cast some light on this question.

The exogenous growth model takes the inputs as given. This would be the case if we think that technology is driven by science and is independent of economic incentives. Given exogenous technology and constant returns to scale (CRS), Adam Smith's model of capitalism predicts that growth will be hitchless. In Ricardo's corn model, corn output depends on labor and capital, and velvet output depends on labor. Labor is paid from a wage fund. Under autarky, changes in the wage fund will lead to expansion of velvet production, lowering its price. However, with trade this need not happen as the world price will dominate (Feenstra 2004, 338). The modern neoclassical production function follows the diminishing returns to production as advanced by Ricardo. The saving will adjust to a constant level of investment, resulting in steady state growth. But, if we fall back on Smith's CRS assumption, and assume that auto output (Y) depends on one factor, say labor (L), then CRS implies that $Y=aL$, where "a" measures the incremental output from one unit of labor and $\Delta Y/\Delta L=a$, implying that doubling L will double Y. Now, if Y is also dependent on both L and capital (K) under CRS production, then doubling all inputs will more than double output, giving increasing returns to scale (IRS). In the domain of the new trade literature, the way technology evolved and is diffused along with CRS and IRS determined the industry's growth rate.

The endogenous growth model holds out help to the modern distressed industries in several ways. These industries need to tie their choices to market incentives that would lead to the production of new technology (Romer 1990, S72). In the long run, their success will depend on "endogenous choices of fiscal policies, foreign trade policies, research and development policies, population policies, and so on" (Bhagwati et al. 1998, 528).

The exogenous growth model seems to be an answer for the distressed industries because it has a huge role for government participation in the area of technology. Research & Development expenditure is a huge concern for the pharmaceutical and auto industries. In the pharmaceutical industry large outlays are necessary because of the length of time and the number of parallel research efforts it takes to produce a new chemical or molecular entity. In the auto industry, each firm strives to bring out a new model every year at substantial expense. In both cases, because firms do not have to compete for the output after it is produced it is classified as a non-rival good, which allows for cooperation among firms and with the government. "As evidence that firms can come together and take actions that are in the interest of the industry as a whole, one need look no further than the pharmaceutical industry. It recently persuaded the Food and Drug Administration (FDA) to raise the fees it levies when a company submits a drug for approval. The explicit understanding was that the FDA would use the additional revenue from this fee to hire more evaluators so that the agency could reduce the time it takes to reach a decision on drug approval (Romer 1993, 352). The government also has lengthened the patent term for drugs to 21 years because it recognizes that it takes a long time to develop a new chemical element (NCE), leaving a short patent time to recover costs. Similarly, the government's role having to make loans to Chrysler has given the car company the breathing room it needed to get abreast of the newer small car technology that the market was signaling at that time. Temporary protection for steel was also necessary for it to be able to compete with NUCOR technology. We are well aware of the strong initiative that is still being made in the area of property rights for the paper and publishing industry. Endogenous growth theory has recognized that R&D expenditures are so paramount in modern growth theories that it has brought them up to the front burner. R&D makes up the first nontraded sector in a modern three sector growth model—the second trade sector purchases the blueprints of the first sector as its fixed cost of production for the production of intermediate goods. The third sector is the final goods sector (Findlay 1995, 71).

Under endogenous growth, inputs such as capital, human resources, and R&D have spilled over nationally and internationally. When a firm invests in these resources, it cannot exhaust all the benefits from them. Some benefits will spill over to other firms, which are likely to find them cheap to imitate. "Firms in the X and Y sectors all benefit jointly from the knowledge generated by the R&D sector, and none can prevent access by other to the same knowledge if they refuse to contribute. The R&D sector, must thus be operated either directly by the government and financed by taxes or as a consortium by the firms" (ibid., 87). In this way, a modern "integrated economy will not only be more productive than an isolated economy but will exhibit a permanently higher growth rate" (Krugman 1994, 167).

Another way to make the same case is to state that, under neoclassical growth models, capital and labor account for only about 15 per cent of the variation of output. This makes technology the residual claimant of the remaining 85 per cent of the growth in output (Findlay 1995, 69–70). Schumpeter argued that firms must take an "exogenous" look at how technology affects growth. Firms take this roundabout way of production by first investing in R&D, which tends to give them a monopoly and high returns. How does this affect gains from trade? First, the broader markets will generate greater returns. Second, as the knowledge diffuses or spills over, or when knowledge is no longer private, all production will take place with better innovation (Krugman 1994, 165). In general, the old tradition credits factor accumulation with over 50 per cent of growth. The newer tradition emphasizes "openness" and "catch-up" effects. By being open, an industry can find new sources for raw materials so that material and labor costs will be lowered (Dornbusch and Edwards 1995, 3 and 17).

Appendix

Statements of the Theorems of Free Trade versus Protectionism

We state the theorems of free trade and protectionism without proof for completeness.

On Free Trade
Adam Smith:

1) "It is the maxim of prudent master of a family, never to attempt to make at home what it will cost him more to make than to buy.... What is prudence in the conduct of every private family, can scarce be folly in that of a great kingdom. If a foreign country can supply us with a commodity cheaper than we ourselves can make it, better buy it of them with some part of the produce of our own industry, employed in a way in which we have some advantage" (Smith 1976, 456–7).
2) "In every country it always is and must be the interest of the great body of the people to buy whatever they want of those who sell it cheapest. The proposition is so very manifest, that it seems ridiculous to take any pains to prove it; nor could it ever have been called in question, had not the interested sophistry of merchants and manufacturers confounded the common sense of mankind" (Smith 1976, 493–4).
3) It is true "that trade which without force or constraint, is naturally and regularly carried on between any two places is always advantageous, though not always equally so, to both... Almost all countries exchange with one another partly native and partly foreign goods. That country, however, in whose cargoes there is the greater proportion of native, and the least of foreign gooods, will always be the principal gainer" (Smith 1996, 489–90).
4) "A nation that would enrich itself by foreign trade is certainly most likely to do so when its neighbours are all rich, industrious, and commercial nations. A great nation surrounded on all sides by wandering savages and poor barbarians might, no doubt, acquire riches by the cultivation of its own lands, and by its own interior commerce, but not by foreign trade" (Smith 1976, 495).

David Ricardo:

1) "Under a system of perfectly free commerce, each country naturally devotes its capital and labor to such employments as are most beneficial to each. This pursuit of individual advantage is admirable connected with the universal good of the whole. By stimulating industry, by rewarding ingenuity, and by using most efficaciously the peculiar powers bestowed by nature, it distributes labor most effectively and most economically: while, by increasing the general mass of productions, it diffuses general benefits, and binds together by one common tie of interest and intercourse, the universal society of nations throughout the civilized world" (Ricardo 1926, 81).

He (Ricardo) showed that the advantage of an interchange of commodities between nations consists simple and solely in this, that it enables each to obtain, with a given amount of labour and capital, a greater quantity of all commodities taken together. This it accomplishes by enabling each, with a quantity of one commodity which has cost it so much labour and capital, to purchase a quantity of another commodity which, if produced at home, would have required labour and capital to a greater amount (Mill 1967, 233).

It should be clarified that the Ricardian theorem holds that "a country will export that commodity in which it has comparative labor productivity advantage" (Bhagwati et al. 1998, 9). It assumes one factor of production, two countries, two goods, no transportation cost, and factor mobility. Adding more countries yields this additional prediction:

2) *(many countries)* "If all countries are ranked according to their labor-productivity ratios, $(Q_1/L_1)/(Q_2/L_2)$, the country with the highest ratio will export good 1, the country with the lowest ratio will import good 1. Countries in the intermediate range may export or import good 1, although all countries exporting good 1 will have higher labor productivity ratios than all countries importing good 1" (Bhagwati et al. 1998, 35).

3) *(many goods)* "If every good is ranked according to its comparative labor-productivity advantages as between the two countries, $$\frac{(Q_1/L_1) > (Q_2/L_2) > (Q_3/L_3)}{(Q_1/L_1)* \ (Q_2/L_2)* \ (Q_3/L_3)*}$$ then each country must export the good in which it has the greatest comparative advantage" (Bhagwati et al. 1998, 41).

Eli Heckscher—Bertil Ohlin (HO):

1) Each country will export the good that uses its abundant factor intensively (Feenstra 2004, 32).

2) "Of two countries, I and II, let I be K-abundant so that $(K/L) > (K/L)*$. Let 1 be the K-intensive good and 2 be the L-intensive good at all factor price ratios so that $k_1 > k_2$ at every ω. Then we know from the Rybczynski theorem that country I will have the advantage in the production of good 1: $(Q_1/Q_2) > (Q_1/Q_2)*$ at all good-price ratios (when incomplete specialization obtains)" (Bhagwati et al. 1998, 79).

3) "Thus, given balanced trade, in the two-factor, many-goods world the capital-labor ratio in a million dollar's worth of exports is larger than the capital-labor ratio in a million dollar's worth of imports. This is precisely the test Leontief applied" (Bhagwati et al. 1998, 121).

Paul A. Samuelson:

Under conditions suitable for perfect competition, free trade is efficient in the sense of wiping out *global deadweight loss*. If you deviate from free trade, those who gain from so doing gain less than those who lose —in the sense that the losers can afford to bribe the winners to desist from protectionism (Samuelson 1986, Volume 5, 511).

Samuelson advanced the idea that "the introduction of outside (relative) prices differing from those which would be established in our economy in isolation will result in some trade, and as a result every individual will be better off than he would be at the prices which prevailed in the isolated state (Samuelson 1966, Volume 2, 786). The subsequent works of Murray Kemp (1962), and Kemp and Henry Wan, Jr. (1972) offer a proof of this situation. The argument in brief is that, if conditions of constant returns to scale, convex production possibilities, and perfect competition prevail, then domestic production minus consumption must be equalized for equilibrium. However, adding that free trade also prevails, then that equality need not hold. It will require that the value of exports must also equal the value of imports. There is implied need for good policy for the external and internal economies.

Samuelson's Le Chatelier principle explains how an economic system that is in equilibrium will react to a perturbation. It predicts that the system will respond in a manner that will counteract the peturbation. Samuelson, who follows the methods of the hard sciences, has transported this principle of chemist Henri-Louis Le Chatelier to economics to study the response of agents to price changes, given some additional constraints. In his extension of this principle, Samuelson uses the metaphor of squeezing a balloon to further explain the concept. If you squeeze a balloon, its volume will decrease more if you keep its temperature constant than it will if you let the squeezing warm it up (Samuelson 1960, 368). This principle is now considered a standard tool for comparative static analysis in economic theory.

On Protectionism
Adam Smith:

> There seem, however, to be two cases in which it will generally be advantageous to lay some burden upon foreign, for the encouragement of domestic industry ... The first is when some particular sort of industry is necessary for the defence of the country ... The second ... is, when some tax is imposed at home upon the produce of the latter. In this case, it seems reasonable that an equal tax should be imposed upon the produce of the former (Smith 1976, 463 and 465).

Friedrich List:

> The (classical) school fails to perceive that under a system of perfectly free competition with more advanced manufacturing nations, a nation which is less advanced than those, although well fitted for manufacturing, can never attain to a perfectly developed manufacturing power of its own, nor to perfect national independence, without protective duties (List 1841, 316).

Jagdish Bhagwati:

1) In the presence of market failures (or distortions), free trade is not necessarily the best policy (Bhagwati 2002, 61).

2) (a) Where the distortion is domestic, a domestic (tax-cum-subsidy) policy targeting will be appropriate and free trade can then be restored as a suitable first-best trade policy; (b) where the distortion is external, free trade must be departed from as part of the suitable first best policy addressed to the distortion (ibid., 61).

In modern literature, several changes in the economy seem to beckon protectionist measures. A collection of some of those reasons include the frequent recurrence of recession, the new structure of international trade—in new industrial countries, steel and automobiles have been important sources of economic stabilization in terms of the employment they provide, and the demand they create for raw materials, failure to adjust to changes in the economic environment, new technologies have brought new issues with economies of scale. Markets may clear at dis-equilibrium prices, which sends the wrong signals, high dependence on energy may lead to cooperative pricing; and debt problems may require institutional changes (Chichilnisky and Heal 1986, 2–5).

Paul Krugman:

> Given the symmetry, full employment and market-clearing conditions require $L = n(\alpha+\beta x)$ and $x = cL$, respectively. These are two equations in three variables x, c, and n. Fixing any one of the variables determines the remaining variables. Alternatively, we need a third equation. Under the behavioral assumption made by Krugman, this condition comes from the firm's profit maximization behavior requiring marginal revenue equal to marginal cost pricing $[p(\varepsilon-1)/\varepsilon=\beta w]$ and free entry leading to average-cost pricing $[p=(\alpha/x)w +\beta w]$ (Bhagwati et al. 1998, 184).

In Krugman's model, α is fixed cost, β is marginal cost, x is output, c is consumption, w is wage, n is the number of varieties, and L is individuals in the economy each supplying a unit of labor. Symmetry exists in production and consumption, implying that price and outputs are similar. Each firm produces a different product. Output, x, and prices, p, are determined where MR=MC, i.e. $p(\varepsilon-1)/\varepsilon=\beta w$. So the ratio of prices of goods relative to wages, p/w, can be inverse when ε declines with c, or direct when average cost pricing is used. These two curves determine c and p/w. We determine $x = cL$, and varieties $n = L/(\alpha+\beta)x^*$.

Krugman's model purports to show that "trade need not be a result of international differences in technology or factor endowment. Instead, trade may simply be a way of extending the market and allowing exploitation of scale economies, with the effects of trade being similar to those of labor force growth and regional agglomeration" (Krugman 1994, 21).

Chapter 2

Global Competition and Policy Analysis: Trade Adjustment Assistance

TAA Benefits in Distressed United States Industries Before and After NAFTA

In the aftermath of NAFTA, and the pending arrival of FTA, Trade Adjustment Assistance (TAA) for distressed United States industries has become a necessary, if not sufficient, policy to relieve the adverse impacts of displaced businesses and workers due to import competition. Over the past two decades, TAA petitions have been filed with the United States Department of Labor by the steel, paper and publishing, footwear, pharmaceutical, garment, and automobile industries. The average number of workers affected each year during the period 1980–1999 was 186,794. However, the arguments persist that free trade creates more jobs than it destroys, that total surplus is made up of consumer surplus and producer surplus, that when one falls the other gains, and that gains are enhanced from trade. Indeed, when we contrast the performance of distressed industries to the performance of the United States economy we find that the overall welfare gain as a result of the breaking down of the barriers of tariffs, quotas, or voluntary restraints between trading partners is large, net of TAA benefits.

The TAA program began in 1962, when United States firms and workers suffered transitional injury due to the impact of increased imports. The program continues today because it acts as a vehicle for distributional equity, allocative efficiency, and as a means to mollify political opposition against trade liberalization. It is active in conjunction with two other labor market programs: the Unemployment Insurance (UI) program that provides job training and placement, counseling, and subsidies for job search expenses, and the Job Training Partnership Act (JIPA) program that provides job search and training assistance to permanently displaced workers that are laid off for reasons unrelated to import impact (Hufbauer and Schott 1992). Also, United States firms may receive after-tax incentives and loan subsidies (Richardson 1982, 324–5). The TAA program was reformed in 1974 when the Trade Act of 1974 loosened eligibility requirements and raised supplements from 65 to 70 per cent of income. The incubation of trade liberalization policies was pregnant with the threat of sanctions to prevent transshipment of foreign goods to the United States via Mexico (*US Industrial Outlook* 1994). However, early setbacks were surmounted by the advent of NAFTA in 1993, and the subsequent related agreements such as the North American Agreement on Environmental

Cooperation (NAAEC), the North American Agreement on Labor Cooperation (NAALC), and the North American Agreement on Import Surges.

The relevance of the TAA is a function of escape clauses in Article XIX of the General Agreement on Tariffs and Trade (GATT) and Sections 201 through 203 of the US Trade Act of 1974. Those escape clauses allow individuals and firms to seek temporary protection from import competition that trade liberalization tends to elevate. Both protection and liberalization have virtues and vices. Protection allows a firm to regroup but ultimately drives up costs (Matsuyama 1990, 480). This study, which covers TAA's performance in several industries during the 1980–1997 sample period, presents a model, implications, and a "but for TAA" estimates of benefits associated with the TAA.

Depending on how an industry adopts to global changes, it can suffer more than others. For example, a total of 355,471 workers in the garment industry and 68,181 workers in the steel industry were certified between 1980 through 1999, and a total of 110,076, and 214,340 workers, respectively, were denied benefits. About one third to one half of the certified and denied workers during the 1994-1999 time period claimed to be displaced because of NAFTA. Using a CGE model to measure the impact of globalization on the garment industry reveals benefits to the United States of approximately $2.5 billion in 1997. Similar analysis indicates that the steel industry gained approximately $21.5 billion in welfare benefits to the United States in 1997, and the automobile industry gained $13.614 billion in 1997. The footwear and paper and publishing industries also gained, as will be shown in later chapters.

Descriptive Statistics

Our tests use a 20-year series of data related to the TAA provided by the United States Department of Labor. The series is available by SIC industry classification, and is further segmented by affected workers, petitions certified, and petitions denied. Table 2.1 presents descriptive statistics for the aggregate series, while Table 2.2 shows disaggregation by year, industry, and FTA influences. From Table 2.1, we note that the number of certified and denied workers was, on average, 186,794 persons per year, with 93,276 certified and 93,518 denied.

The prefixes C and D refer to certified and denied, respectively. PETI is short for petition. Table 2.2 presents statistics about TAA petitions that were filed and the number of employees that were affected for the set of distressed industries. The data is presented for two subperiods, before and after NAFTA. We further tabulate certifications and denials for petitions and workers identified as being related to NAFTA.

Table 2.2 indicates that although the number of petitions in the paper and publishing industry was small, the number of employees affected totaled in the thousands, with 4,028 employees certified and 8,147 denied. We notice that after every FTA the number of petitions representing the number of workers affected, is

Table 2.1 Descriptive statistics, 1980–1999

Variable	Count	Mean	Std. dev.	Std. dev. of mean
CPETI	20	804.7500	351.3943	78.57416
CWORK	20	93275.60	120021.1	26837.52
DPETI	20	801.2500	543.1972	121.4626
DWORK	20	93517.50	67738.70	15146.83

larger than during non FTA periods. The implication is as expected: the industry suffered due to free competition. The distinction between per cent certified and denied in the pre and post FTA periods is not compelling. For instance, there is no evidence that the per cent of petitions denied after the liberalization effort has decreased. FTA's do not lead to a lower denial percentage in TAA benefits. Only after NAFTA did the percentage of employees denied TAA benefits decrease from 9.53 to 6.39 per cent. While the affected number of employees is large relative to the industry, it does not influence the nation's employment or political agenda. Szenberg and Lee (1994) argue that the book industry, in particular, is a "for-profit" business, letting the private sector primarily absorb the shock.

The statistics show that over the 1980–1998 period pharmaceutical companies filed only 28 petitions with the ITC. These petitions, which cover 4,535 employees, were mostly denied (20 with 3,906 workers), though a few were approved (8 with 629 workers). The small import impact may be attributed to the pharmaceutical companies' longstanding wariness towards foreign competition, which led them to utilize other strategies such as drug licensing.

Table 2.2 shows that the number of petitions in the footwear industry changed about 6 per cent across the pre- and post-NAFTA years. The corresponding employee annual percentages also tracked a similar trend. The precipitous change in the percentage of denials for the corresponding before and after trade liberalization periods is notable; the NAFTA period experienced an approximately 7 to 2 per cent drop in denials of petitions.

The auto industry experienced the largest number of workers certified during the 1980–1999 period, 600,653. The second largest was the garment industry with 355,471 workers. The third largest was the steel industry with 68,181 workers.

Unit Root Test

The TAA data is unique and is generally used in cross-section, not in a time-series analysis as performed in this investigation. We are therefore interested in its stationarity properties, because if it is nonstationary, regression results can be spurious. This means that t-values and R-squares can be inflated because

Table 2.2 **Petitions and employment experiences of various free trade hypotheses, 1980–1999**

Years	Petitions				Workers			
	Total certified	Total denied	Annual % certified	Annual % denied	Total certified	Total denied	Annual % certified	Annual % denied
1 **Steel**: SIC 3312–3399, 1980–99	509	1141			68181	214340		
Data for NAFTA Comparison:								
Total: 1980–93	403	1065	6.09	7.18	51760	207279	5.84	12.82
Total: 1994–99	106	76	4.17	1.33	16421	7061	4.82	1.14
NAFTA: 1994–99	39	29			5938	3914		
2 **Paper & Pub.**: SIC 2711–2799, 1980–99	32	86			4028	8147		
Data for NAFTA comparison:								
Total: 1980–93	12	36	2.68	2.99	1341	4505	2.38	3.95
Total: 1994–99	20	50	8.93	8.31	2687	3642	9.53	6.39
NAFTA: 1994–99	16	16			1730	199		
3 **Drugs**: 1980–99	8	20			629	3906		
Data for NAFTA comparision:								
Total: 1980–93								
Total: 1994–99								
NAFTA: 1994–99								
4 **Footwear**: 1980–99	574	269			56076	18005		
Data for NAFTA comparison:								
Total: 1980–93	411	242	5.51	6.92	38615	16576	5.30	7.08
Total: 1994–99	163	27	5.68	2.01	17461	1429	6.23	1.59
NAFTA: 1994–99								
5 **Garment**: 1980–99	3,791	1,783			355,471	110,076		
Data for NAFTA comparison:								
Total: 1980–93	2,034	1,633			168,072	100,040		
Total: 1994–99	1,757	150			187,419	10,036		
Nafta: 1994–99								
6 **Autos**: 1980–99								
1980–99	840	1,447			600,653	332,110		
Data for NAFTA comparison								
1980–93	753	1,373			587,264	323,093		
1994–99	87	74			13,389	9,017		

regression analysis would superimpose information on the estimated coefficients for variables that also affect the dependent variables besides the ones we included (Studenmund 1997, 489).

Figures 2.1 and 2.2 provide plots of the TAA series. These plots demonstrate that the series tend to move in trend and cycles over time. Figure 2.1 indicates that certified workers (CWORK) decreased significantly in 1981. A study at that time noted that a "majority of TAA clients had gone back to their old jobs, that most were back at work when they collected TRAs, and that training and relocation services were scarcely used, made TAA a prime target for cost cutting as the Reagan Administration took office in 1981" (US Congress 1987, 26). Post–1981 we see a stable period of certified workers, and even a declining trend in the denials (DWORK). Similar time trends are displayed for number of petitions certified (CPETI), and denied (DPETI).

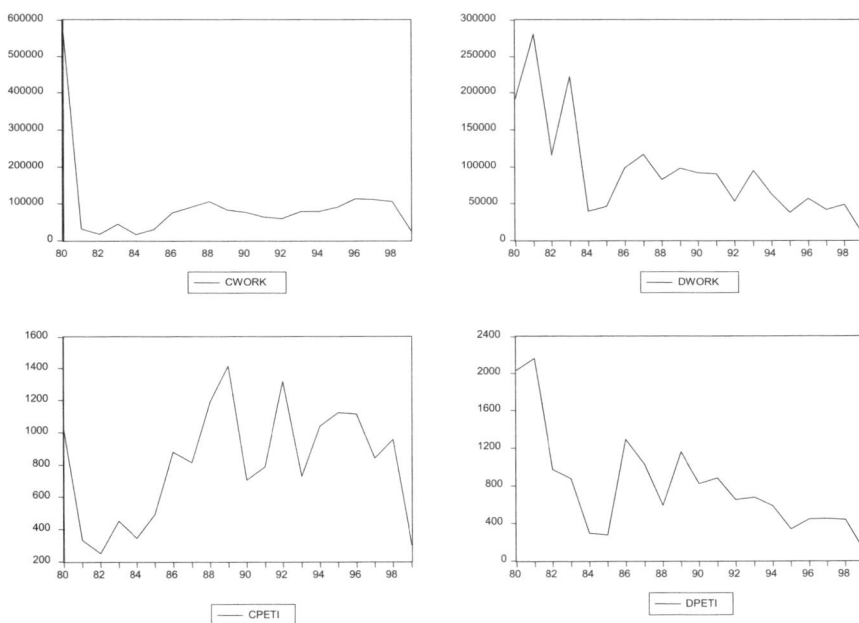

Figure 2.1   Plot of the numbers of workers and petitions approved and denied TAA 1960–1999

A major hypothesis that we investigate is whether imports have had a causal influence on these variable. After all TAA is designed to assist workers and businesses that are impacted by imports. Since the OPEC crisis in 1973, imports of foreign cars have reduced the market share of domestic automobile firms. Free Trade Agreements such as NAFTA, CAFTA, and ISFTA have competed away benefits of the domestic footwear, textile and wearing apparels, and other

American industries. Imports are therefore seen as a causal link to TAA benefits. In our endeavor to sort out causal relationships, we do not assume that one method dominates another. For instance, Hoover (2001, 155) indicated that the popular Granger causality is "neither necessary nor sufficient for structural causality in a range of cases important to macroeconomics." Since we perform structural analyses in different contexts, such as in establishing elasticities and in assessing the influence of imports and exports on TAA affected workers or number of petitions filed at the Department of Labor for TAA benefits, we do not necessarily need to appeal to the whole set of relevant information that applies to global trading, but only to "a more limited set of *relevant* factors" (ibid., 150).

But regression analysis can overstate relevant relationships. Suppose FTAs shock the economic system. Then TAA can come to the system's rescue if the shocks dissipate. A classical method through which to specify such a model would be to follow a known established specification. For instance, we can follow Kuh and Schmalensee (1972, 99) and fit an equation that follows Koyck distributed lag form: $Import_t = f (GDP_t, Relative\ prices_t, Import_{t-1})$. However, the modern literature would not accommodate such an analysis if the data are spurious. The literature recommends that we must achieve some "balance" before the regression analysis is undertaken (Granger 1999, 18). Balance implies that some level of comparable order will be built into the data. For instance, Figure 2.2 indicates that a plot of GDP follows an upward trend, and a plot of relative prices a downward trend, both with smaller cycles than the TAA data indicates. Although it recognizes that we can never be sure that GNP is an integrated series, the literature suggests that "modeling GNP as an integrated process seems to provide a good approximation to its long-run properties" (Stock and Watson 1991, 23).

We next determine whether the TAA series and the other variables such as imports are integrated or cointegrated. In traditional research, we refer to two series as collinear if they move in the same trend and cycle. In his Nobel Prize lecture, Granger used a "two necklaces" metaphor. If we place two necklaces on a table, we may find that the distance between them is similar. The comparisons may be done on a bead-for-bead basis, but we should not interpret 'similar' to mean 'exact.' We may use an analogy to an owner walking his/her dog. They are tied together by a cord, but the distance between the owner and the dog may be allowed to vary as the owner draws-inward or releases the cord. The literature has used vague concepts such as collinearity or underlining tendency towards a long-run equilibrium to characterize such relationships in the past. With Granger, such cointegration relationships are central to our analysis. If series are cointegrated, we may apply an error corrective mechanism (ECM) model to reset them when they deviate.

We begin by investigating whether our TAA and imports series over time, and by industry, states, etc., are nonstationary to the same degree, as indicated by I(0) or I(1) for level or first differences. If they are both random walk models, then through combining or cointegrating them, for example through letting z =

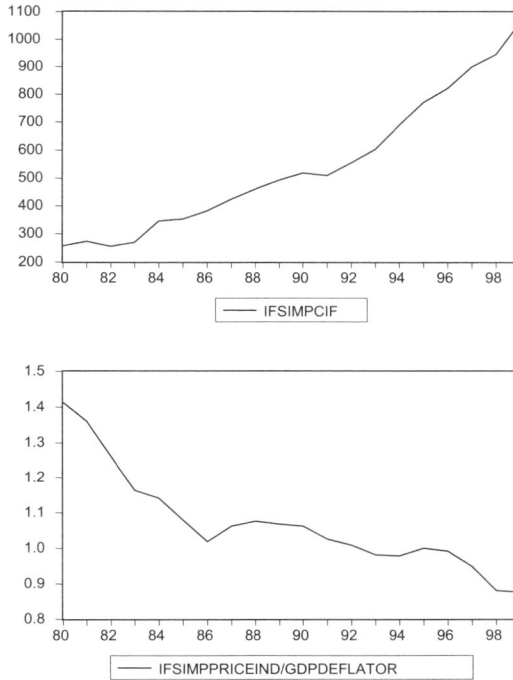

Figure 2.2   Independent variables (GNP) and relative prices

imports – beta * TAA, their spuriousness may cancel out each other (Pindyck and Rubinfeld 1998, 513).

We begin with the simple assumption that the TAA series gradually increases over time. Consider a random process, $y_t - y_{t-1} = c + e_t$, where y is TAA, c is a constant, e is a random error term, and t is time. The simple Dickey-Fuller Unit Root test for stationarity requires us to regress y_t on constant c, a lag value of the dependent variable y_{t-1}. The distinction is made between a random walk and an integrated model. In the former, no autocorrelation of the error terms is allowed. In the latter, the error term is stationary but can correlate with lagged error terms (Stock and Watson 1991, 22). If the coefficient of the lagged value of the dependent variable is in the interval $(-1, 1)$, then y_t is considered stationary. If it is one, then the series is nonstationary. If it exceeds one, the series is explosive, which typically does not figure into economic analysis. For example, in the case of first differences, we test the one tail test, H_0: coefficient $=1$, against the alternative, H_1: coefficient <1. Since we work in first differences, our AR(1) process becomes $\Delta y_t = c + (p-1)y_{t-1} + e_t$. So the estimate of the lagged variable is p–1. Therefore, after establishing first differences, we are testing H_0: coefficient $= 0$ against the alternative H_1: coefficient <0.

Table 2.3 displays the results for our test of stationarity of the certified workers and petitions under the TAA program for 1980 to 1999. The equation we test is:

$$Y_t = a + b.\,\text{Time} + p.Y_{t-1} + e_t$$

We are interested in situations where we can use the series represented by the dependent variable (Y) in its actual form in traditional regression analysis such as OLS. This would be the case where we have a trend (significant b), and stationary after detrending (p < 1) (Pindyck and Rubinfeld 1998, 507). The one tail test leads us to reject the null hypothesis if the ADF statistic is to the right of the critical statistic. The results presented in Table 2.3 show the results for certified workers and petitions using first differences and no differences (I(1) and I(0)), along with an intercept and trend. While the t-values are significant, they are not used in the stationarity test. The MacKinnon critical values are used for all sample sizes for stationarity determination. In all cases the ADF statistic is to the right of the critical values, implying that we cannot reject the null hypothesis. Therefore, we cannot tell whether the series are stationary, hence we use them with caution. For certified workers, the ADF statistic is not to the right of the critical MacKinnon values in the last two columns, since the null hypothesis is the presence of unit root. Thus, the augmented Dickey-Fuller statistics all lie inside the acceptance region at 1 per cent or 5 per cent. We cannot then reject the presence of unit root, implying that we cannot be sure of stability.

Table 2.3   Level, I(0) and first difference, I(1) of TAA data, 1980–1999

Description	Parameter	Y=CWORK I(0) with u and trend	Y=CPETI I(0) with u and trend	Y=CWORK I(1) with u and trend	Y=CPETI I(1) with u and trend
Constant	a	321888.78 (2.77)***	394.98 (1.88)**	23599.59 (1.55)	175.96 (0.94)
Trend	b	3266.77 (2.30)***	20.02 (1.20)	-2118.85 (1.66)	−17.02 (−1.06)
ADF statistics	p	−1.0 (−18.48)***	−0.76 (−2.76)***	−0.94 (−18.41)***	−1.27 (−5.38)***
R^2		0.96	−0.33	−0.97	0.68
Critical value @ .01%		−4.53	-4.53	−4.57	−4.57
Critical value @ .05%		−3.67	-3.67	−3.69	−3.69
Sample period		1981–1999	1981–1999	1982–1999	1982–1999

A General Equilibrium Framework for TAA

The TAA model can be placed within the Second Welfare Theorem that considers welfare optimum after transfers such as TAA. Empirically, TAA data is available in time-series and cross-sectional form that allows for both partial equilibrium (PE) and computational general equilibrium (CGE) tests. The partial equilibrium approach examines the conventional effect that trade liberalization has in expanding the area of measuring consumer surplus. The resulting welfare gains, based on prevalent tariff rates, price elasticity, and value of imports, is netted to allow for estimates of costs to the displaced employees. The general equilibrium approach that compares NAFTA countries with the rest of the world (ROW) permits us to reconcile the PE and CGE estimates, which adjust for substitution and distortions both among and within industries.

The use of TAA in both the PE and CGE assessments of TAA's influence on distressed industries has a positive influence on welfare benefits of the industry during the trade liberalization era. The twin estimations show a robust view of TAA performance. TAA cushions distress to displaced workers and minimizes transition costs to other job placements or retirement, while allowing for increased efficiency due to liberalized trade.

Models of TAA are subsumed under the Second Welfare Theorem in economics. Empowered by the Trade Acts of 1962 and 1974, TAA represents a subsidy or transfer payments of money, not goods and services, to displaced workers in import-impacted industries. In theory, the dichotomy between money and goods and services makes a difference in welfare enhancement to the equilibrium of an economy. In technical jargon, the allocation of goods and services by the government, rather than money, prevents a market from attaining Pareto optimal allocation of resources.

Following Feenstra and Lewis (1994), the theoretical literature accounts for TAA via a production function that transfers factors across industries within an Arrow-Debreu framework. Models vary depending on the assumptions placed on prices and factors. Assuming autarky prices for consumers and free trade prices for producers, Dixit and Norman (1980, 1986) argue for Pareto optimality with less information than is demanded in the transfer function model but with commodity taxation and poll subsidy. Feenstra and Lewis (1994) will consider moving factors only with incentives such as provided by TAA. In other words, their model assumes that factors are imperfectly mobile to begin with, which must be augmented with an incentive for factors to move. However, their model does not conform to the TAA rules. Instead, they trade off relocation subsidies with factor subsidies, making TAA incentive rather than benefit based. They further assume a continuum of each type of individual, and allow no labor-leisure choice. To incorporate the various ways in which TAA benefits are paid, we present a more theoretic encapsulation of welfare models under the first and second welfare theorems, as follows.

Assumption 1

A = a set of agents.
a = an individual in the set of agents.
$\geq_a$ = agent a's preference.
e(a) = agent a's endowment.
t: A ® R = TAA income transfer function.
p = prices.
x = commodities.
{ x| p.x ≤ pe } = individual budget set without TAA benefits.
{ x| p.x ≤ pe + t(a) } = budget set of displaced employees receiving TAA benefits.
f(a) = agent a's maximizing preference over its budget set.

Proposition 1

Without trade liberalization, Walrasian equilibrium is achieved when the sum of all agents' preferences are less than or equal to all their endowment, i.e., $\{\Sigma_{a\in A} f(a) \leq \Sigma_{a\in A} e(a)\}$.

Proposition 1 is traditionally discussed in the literature under the First Welfare Theorem, and a simple proof in terms of core theory exists. If x represents an allocation and e the agent's initial endowment, then the solution set, F(e), has the property that the sum of the total allocations is equal to or less than the sum of the total endowments $F(e) = [x | \Sigma_{a\in A} f(a) \leq \Sigma_{a\in A} e(a)]$. A Pareto optimal core exists if (1) x is in F(e), (2) xa ≥a ea, and (3) y is in F(e), where y ≠ x, such that y does not block x. The proof is by contradiction: Suppose not. Then ∃y in F(e), where y ≠ x, such that y blocks x, implying that x is not in the core, a contradiction.

Proposition 2

With trade liberalization, in spite of the impact on imports, Walrasian equilibrium is achieved when the sum of all the agents' preferences are less than or equal to all their endowments plus TAA benefits, i.e.,$[\Sigma_{a\in A} f(a) \leq \Sigma_{a\in A} e(a) + t(a)]$.

Proof of Proposition 2 is more complex, requiring nonstandard analysis or measure theory (See Kreps 1990, and Aliprantis et al. 1990). We limit our analysis of this proposition to the case of quasi-equilibrium, where some agents may have zero income at the supporting equilibrium prices. These results are found in the following modified proposition.

Proposition 2A

If f is Pareto optimal, then there is an income transfer t and p ≠ 0, such that (f,p) ∈ Q(x,t), and for p >>0, $\Sigma_{a\in A}$ t(a) = 0, such that (f,p) ∈ W(x,t),

Assumption 2

X: A ® P x R^k_+ is an exchange economy, where A is a finite set, and P represents all binary preferences relations on the space R^k_+.

$\geq_a$ is now made convex, strongly monotone, and locally nonsatiated for all a.

$\Sigma_{a \in A}$ e(a) >>0.

An allocation is a function α :A ® R^k_+, such that $\Sigma_{a \in A}$ α(a) = $\Sigma_{a \in A}$ e(a).

A Weak allocation is a function α· such that $\Sigma_{a \in A}$ α(a) $\leq$ $\Sigma_{a \in A}$ e(a).

A Pareto optimal allocation is a function α, such that there is no other allocation β, such that β (a) $\geq_a$ α (a) for all a∈A.

A TAA transfer is a function t: A∈ R such that: $\Sigma_{a \in A}$ t(a) < 0.

Definitions

Demand: D(p,a,t) = {x in R^k_+ | px $\leq$ pe(a) + t(a), y $>_a$ x implies that py > pe(a) + t(a)}

Quasi Demand: Q(p,a,t) = {x in R^k_+ | px $\leq$ pe(a) + t(a), y $>_a$ x implies that py $\geq$ pe(a) + t(a)}

Excess Demand: E(p,a,t) = [d –e(a)| d $\in$ D(p,a,t)]

Walrasian: W(x,t) = {α, p| α: A ® R^k, $\Sigma_{a \in A}$ α(a) = $\Sigma_{a \in A}$ e(a), α (a) $\in$ D(p,a,t), for all a $\in$ A}

Quasi Equilibrium: Q(x, t) = {α, p|α: A ® R^k, $\Sigma_{a \in A}$ α(a) $\leq$ $\Sigma_{a \in A}$ e (a), α (a) $\in$ Q(p,a,t), for all a $\in$ A] }

Proof {Quasi Equilibrium}

Let f be Pareto optimal. Let Q(a) = {x – f(a)| x $>_a$ f(a)}.

Then M = $\Sigma_{a \in A}$ M(a) is convex because M(a) is convex.

And 0 $\notin$ M because f is Pareto optimal.

So, there exists a price, p $\neq$ 0, p.0 $\leq$ *inf* (pM) by Minkowski's Theorem.

By local nonsatiation, *inf* (p.M(a)) $\leq$ 0,

inf (p.M) = $\Sigma_{a \in A}$ *inf* (p.M(a))

So, *inf* (p.M(a)) = 0 for all a.

Now, x $>_a$ f(a) implies that p(x-f(a)) $\geq$ 0

Which in turn implies that px $\geq$ f(a).

If we make all f(a) affordable to the agents by:

Letting t(a) = p{f(a) –e(a)}

Solve for: pf(a) = pe(a) + t(a)

So, x $>_a$ f(a) implies that px $\geq$ pf(a) = pe(a) + t(a)

So, f(a) is in Q(p,a,t). Q.E.D.

In the TAA model above we assume that all income transfers to displaced workers in the import-impacted garment industry are TAA benefits. A modification would place an upper bound on the transfer function to reflect an appropriate benefit period. This would address a critical item in the 1962 and 1974 Acts where 52 weeks of payments was the general rule, and 65 weeks in 1962 increased to 78 weeks in 1974, though people over the age of 60 were excluded from this change. A second modification imputes values to other in-kind benefits such as job training and counseling, and other cash benefits such as job search allowances and relocation payments. Both the 1962 and 1974 Acts were somewhat miserly on in-kinds benefits, limiting it to access to other Federal Programs. The 1962 Act had no job search benefit, but an amount limited to $500 was put in place by the 1974 Act. A trade-off in the benefits provided occurred between 1962 and 1974 for relocation payments. The 1962 Act allowed all relocation and necessary expenses plus two and a half times the average weekly manufacturing wages; the 1974 Act, 80 per cent of the former, and three times the worker's own average weekly wage. It would be possible to define other transfer functions to represent these cases. It suffices to say that a simple approach would be to replicate the above model for each of the benefits identified. Our study assumes this latter approach.

The above two propositions provide the basis for our investigation of TAA's impact on the economy. Specifically, we investigate the trade liberalization impact on several industries and all of the other sectors for the NAFTA countries. Such an equilibrium viewpoint grants insight into the net consumer and producer surpluses, employment gains or losses, and any efficiency that may result from the elimination of less competitive production technologies, while allowing TAA subsidies to ease the transition process. Several specifications advanced in the next section facilitate the calculation.

Chapter 3

The Footwear Industry

Introduction and Overview

Between 1994–1999, the early years of the Clinton administration's experience with NAFTA, 163 petitions covering 17,461 employees were certified for the footwear industry.[1] This is in sharp contrast with the early 1962–1969 period when no petitions for tariff adjustment or for assistance to firms and workers were granted. Up to 1974 when 118 petitions affecting 30,000 workers in the footwear industry were filed, only 43 were certified (Szenberg et al. 1977, 122). Table 3.1 details the empirical data for that period.

A salient feature of Table 3.1 is the apparent stability of the annual percentages for petitions and employees certified in the periods before and after trade liberalization. The number of petitions changed about 6 per cent for the pre- and post-NAFTA years, 5 per cent for the United States-Canada-FTA years, and 6 to 7 per cent for the United States-Israel-FTA years. The corresponding employee annual percentages also tracked a similar trend. The big surprise is the precipitous change in the percentage of denials for the corresponding before and after trade liberalization periods. The NAFTA period experienced about a 7 to 2 per cent drop in denials of petitions, and for the FTA areas, from about a 10:4 in petitions up to a 16:3 per cent drop in employees.

A 1977 study by Szenberg et al., provided a comprehensive survey of TAA benefits for the shoe industry in relation to OMA, United States-Israel, and United States-Canada FTA's. In addition to giving the history, evolution and rationale of TAA benefits, that study developed a partial equilibrium (PE) methodology, and estimated that the elimination of the tariff rate by 10 per cent would yield an approximate $78.69 million in net social welfare gain to consumers. A 1982 study by Richardson (1982, 350) also uses a PE methodology to underscore benefits from TAA. Along with the apparel and auto industries, it found that TAA recipients

---

[1] In 1993, a failed attempt by the footwear industry was made to show that import restrictions in the UK, France, Brazil, Taiwan, South Korea, and Japan diverted world export to the United States. We may infer also that if the dramatic dominance of China's share of the market of 72.8 per cent in 1977 versus 5 per cent in 1987 is a result of transshipment, then sanctions would be appropriate. To the extent that United States exports do not counterbalance transshipment activities, the burden to the economy will increase in proportion. Hufbauer et al. (1997) estimated that the burden of sanctions in 1995 could be as high as $19 billion.

Table 3.1   Petitions and employment experience for various free trade hypotheses, 1980–1999

	Petitions				Employees			
Years	Total certified	Total denied	Annual % certified	Annual % denied	Total certified	Total denied	Annual % certified	Annual % denied
1980–99:	574	269			56076	18005		
Data for NAFTA comparison:								
1980–93	411	242	5.51%	6.92%	38615	16576	5.30%	7.08%
1994–99	163	27	5.68%	2.01%	17461	1429	6.23%	1.59%
Data for USISFTA comparison:								
1980–86	247	156	7.17%	9.67%	17854	13563	5.31%	12.55%
1987–99	327	113	4.75%	3.50%	38222	4442	5.68%	2.06%
Data for USCAFTA comparison:								
1980–84	111	139	4.83%	12.92%	9600	11718	4.28%	16.27%
1985–99	463	130	5.76%	3.45%	46476	6287	5.92%	2.49%

Note: Estimated from data provided by the Office of Trade Adjustment Assistance.

in the footwear industry had about seven to 17 weeks per year more favorable employment experience than in other industries.

In a different vein, a 1984 study by Aho and Bayard (1984, 185) tabulated quantitative results of TAA benefits for approximately a 25-year period. Its major premise was to include administrative costs of implementing TAA into benefit calculations. It found that the annual welfare gains from trade liberalization greatly exceeded TAA administrative costs and beneficiary payments. The study did not single out the footwear industry for analysis, but provided estimates for only the leather wearing apparel industry. The International Trade Commission released a May 1999 study with some estimates of NAFTA on the footwear industry (USITC May 1999, Publication 3201). It used a general equilibrium (GE) model to estimate the removal of tariffs to US imports of footwear that would generate about $501 million in welfare gains in 1996 (ibid., 127). This estimate greatly exceeds the $147 million for nonrubber footwear, and $40 million for rubber footwear estimates the USITC present in its 1995 study (USITC December 1995, Publication 2935, 6–5). William E. Spriggs found fault with this wide variation in GE estimate when he said that GE "… need(s) to present policy makers with goodness-of-fit statistics" (USITC May 1992, Publication 2508, 663).

Because of the wide range of the GE benefit estimates, and the unavailability of the ITC data to allow different levels of data aggregation to reconcile its estimate with the PE results, we have decided to adopt the PE methodology developed by Szenberg et al. (1977) to estimate benefits. Most GE analyses use the latest 1996 data from the Global Trade Analysis Project (GTAP) put out by Purdue University staff. However, the footwear industry is not distinguished from the leather industry in GTAP. The USITC has collected some data for the footwear industry, but does not make it available to the public. To get around the data constraint, we have decided to adopt and expand the Szenberg's et al., PE methodology to estimate benefits during the pre- and post-NAFTA periods.

This study is set apart from others in the literature in that it uses time-series data for the 1980 to 1997 period, which was not generally available when the other studies were performed. When such data was used in past studies, it was limited to aggregate assessment of TAA for the whole US economy, and not for specific industries (Hufbauer and Schott 1992, 114–16). In the very few instances in which the benefits to the footwear industry were estimated, cross-section data, which was static for particular years, formed the bases of these estimates (USITC's December 1995, and May 1999 studies). The rest of this chapter is divided into three sections that lay out the model, present the estimates of parameters and benefits, discuss results, simulate welfare benefits, and provide conclusions.

Model

The model will examine the extent to which the TAA assistance would be favorable to the employment situation of displaced workers. In addition, it will shed light on rule-of-thumb measures, such as the frequently cited measure to the effect that 20,000 jobs are lost for every $1 billion worth of new trade generated from trade liberalization. In the case of Mexico, it may explain why the trading of some capital for less illegal immigration may represent an optimal outcome. A central hypothesis we present is that high levels of imports of shoes have overshadowed domestic production, resulting in the displacement of workers, thus establishing the need for the TAA. This hypothesis is stated formally as follows:

> **Proposition 1**: *Lower tariffs lead consumers in the importing country to switch consumption from home to foreign goods, thus increasing imports.*
> **Corollary 1**: *The imports of developing countries such as Mexico are comprised in large part of intermediate goods and services, while those of developed countries such as the U. S. are in the form of final goods and services.*
> **Proposition 2**: *A country can gain from free or even freer trade.*
> **Corollary 2**: *Free or freer trade is imitated in the global economy.*

Proposition 1 is derived from standard textbook arguments. We do not expect consumers to divide their expenditures equally across firms. Similarly, we do not expect the ratio of sales to income in the home and foreign country to be proportionate, as if that were the case, all firms would be involved in international trade (Mussa in Bhagwati 1992, 218). In reality, when trade barriers are lowered, trade is not balanced industry by industry. In particular, we expect protected industries with inefficient use of factor proportions to be most impacted from import surges, leading to lay-offs and the need for TAA. Therefore, we expect import surges consequent to liberalization to require some form of assistance or transfer payments to stay in equilibrium. This expectation is grounded in Walrasian equilibrium models that predicted that the sum of all the agents preference is less than or equal to all their endowment plus TAA benefits and other types of transfer payments.

Corollary 1 is also justified from standard textbook arguments to the extent that trade in factors and goods are substitutes (Mundell 1957). In essence, goods in trade can be viewed as embodying services of factors in trade. In reality, both types of trade in factors and goods are observed, and indeed, both may be necessary to optimize all the gains from trade. This corollary points to the asymmetric arrangement between Mexico and the United States because the latter may be seeking a low-wage partner, while the former may be seeking access to capital goods. Mexico's primary objective could very well be industrialization in which the level of free trade is more beneficial than with protection (Bhagwati 1983, Volume I, 425). Observed from a utility perspective, Mexico's social welfare utility function is now constrained by the policy that would ensure that its employment of labor will not fall below a certain level. This could be achieved by a reallocation of resources in the areas where production was below its free trade optimal point, and not necessarily through a subsidy (ibid., 400–404). The primary objectives of the United States, on the other hand, could be to limit production to its efficient level, which may entail lay-offs in the impacted industry. In that instance, TAA has a role to play.

Proposition 2 underscores the prediction of the traditional paradigm that trade enhances welfare (McFadyen 1988). A standard gravity model,[2] for instance, predicts improved trade (export-import) and welfare benefits for countries sharing a common border and common language (Hufbauer 1997). It suffices to state that from a GE perspective, the countries' position on the Edgeworth contract would be improved. However, the model we will follow is based on the PE foundation set out by Szenberg et al., (1977). This study basically postulated that the area of consumer surplus (CS) increases with trade liberalization and decreases with trade barriers such as tariffs, quotas, or voluntary restraints. We discuss this method in greater detail in the welfare benefit section below.

Corollary 2 links the national analysis with the rest of the world. It has been argued that the formation of FTAs in the world occurs in an imitating fashion. NAFTA may be seen as North America's response to the European's Economic Union. The rationale is that countries tend to make greater economic gains trading with others (group rationality), rather than trading alone (individual rationality). Under those circumstances, US workers may not find it beneficial to voluntarily move from import-impacted industry. They may anticipate more gain from acting as a group and lobby for TAA to absorb the shock of lay-offs.

---

[2]   A gravity model posits a direct relation for output and an inverse relation of distance between countries with trade (Hufbauer et al. 1997, 2). This is a model used for trade theory since the 1960s.

Fung and Staiger (1996) have envisioned the former scenario. In this chapter, we look at the TAA side.

Specifications

We want to specify equations for the model discussed above to bring out statistical links between trade concessions and increased imports and between increased imports and serious injury to workers. The results should help to explain the argument that, but for trade concessions, imports would not have increased. We have two sets of indicators for the goals of TAA, namely, one for the number of petitions certified or denied, and one for the number of workers certified or denied. They are the dependent variables to be explained. We have to choose a set of independent variables to explain them, and specify a linear or non-linear form of the relationship between the dependent and independent variables. For the lack of very specific guidance in the literature, we have opted for the log-linear equations to be estimated.

The equations below are intended to explain how the number of petitions or employees will vary with a measure for increased imports, given other economic and non-economic variables. The traditional economic variables are prices and income, while the noneconomic variables are those that require value-judgment. Eq. 1 explains certification for TAA by income, import prices, import penetration, and plant closings. Among the import penetration measures, the absolute increase in imports itself or the ratio of imports to domestic production has been tested. But the literature has documented that "… it is the rise of imports itself that provides the principal benefits of trade liberalization: with a shift in purchases from high-cost domestic to low-cost foreign merchandise" (Balassa 1967, 72). We have therefore captured the increase in imports via a dummy variable as defined below. *A priori* knowledge would justify a positive coefficient if increased imports dominate exports. A negative import coefficient would be justified if the corresponding increase in exports is not forthcoming, or if domestic producers are making substitutions in their methods of production to absorb the shock of import surges.

To explain denials of TAA, Eq. 2 posits denials in the context of policy initiatives within the sample period of 1980 to 1999. On the one hand, OMA,[3] which expired in 1981, was assigned a dummy of ones from 1981 onwards, but it did not result in singularities in the estimates. On the other hand the omission of the specification of OMA, noted above, is essential for the success of the model. The United States-Israel FTA acted as a pilot study to test the economic principle

---

[3]   OMA was an agreement between the United States, Taiwan, and South Korea to restrict their exports to the United States It succeeded in leveling off import penetration for a while, but its expiration in 1981 caused an upsurge of imports to about 153 per cent (*US Industrial Outlook* 1987, 43–5).

that trade liberalization and duty-free tariffs can work. Perhaps more experience was needed before the United States entertained a zero-border approach, because when the successful USISFTA template was cloned for the United States-Canada FTA, some disagreements surfaced. However, the exploration was over by November 1993 when NAFTA was signed. Because of this dramatic drop in application denials in the trade liberalization years, we have based Eq. 2 on those international agreements, which appear to be the cause of the drop.

Eq. 3 is a production function that accounts for United States productivity effects that have been cited as a potential absorber of trade liberalization shocks to the economy. A production specification would also capture one of the novel effects of the model, namely, that capital will migrate to Mexico as a trade-off for less illegal immigration (Bhagwati 1983). However, the latter would be addressed only indirectly as would the cost of capital in conjunction with labor cost for the calculation of net consumer benefits, the difficulty of which was discussed in Szenberg et al. (1977). It will also capture factor substitutions effects. For instance, "American wage rates have been higher than in the rest of the world, but historically they have been offset by the higher productivity of American labor" (ibid., 118). The wage gap has narrowed somewhat between the United States and Mexico since NAFTA, but the argument still holds true for wage differentials with China (which now has the largest share of United States footwear imports) as well as for Indonesia, North Korea, and Vietnam. American firms have also been substituting "time rate" for "piece rate" in their relatively capital-intensive techniques of production (Freeman and Kleiner 1998). This substitution lowers productivity, but adds some cost savings in insurance, wage monitoring, and inventory.

From another perspective, the productivity argument is necessary because of the "… failure of conventional macro policy to sustain full employment and to ease the re-absorption of displaced resources which has dramatically brought home the fact that import impact is only one of many possible causes of economic dislocation and unemployment" (Szenberg et al. 118). Another issue related to productivity is technological change via both computer-aided design (CAD) and computer-aided manufacturing (CAM). The integration of manufacturing, management, and sales promotion tasks can cut production time and enhance quality, enabling some competition with imports. By explicitly accounting for productivity in our model with TAA, we extend the well-established link of imports to productivity.

$$\text{LCERTIFIED} = a1 + a2\ \text{LPDI Pm} + a4\ \text{Impdum} + a5\ \text{LCLOSING} \quad \text{Eq. 1}$$

$$\text{LDENIALS} = b1 + b2\ \text{NAFTA} + b3\ \text{OMA} + b4\ \text{USISFTA} + b5\ \text{USCAFTA} \quad \text{Eq. 2}$$

$$\text{LVALUE} = c1 + c2\ \text{LLABOR} + c3\ \text{LCAPITAL} \quad \text{Eq. 3}$$

where

CERTIFIED = Number of petitions/employees certified for TAA.
DENIALS = Number of petitions/employees denied TAA.
VALUE = Value of domestic footwear.
PDI = Personal disposable income in constant 1982–84 dollars.
Pm = Import prices in unit value.
Impdum = A dummy of one for years in which import increases.
CLOSING = Plant closings.
NAFTA = A dummy of one for NAFTA 1994 onwards (passed: November 1993).
OMA = A dummy of one for 1977–1981 for the OMA years (expired: 1981).
USISFTA = A dummy of one for 1985 onwards for the United States and Israel FTA.
USCAFTA = A dummy of one for 1988 onwards for the United States and Canada FTA.
L = Log-arithmetic values.

Results

The results corroborate the *a priori* specification of the TAA model. Table 3.2 indicates a preponderance of significant relationships for the number of petitions and benefits to employees' models. We obtained our best results from 3SLS, which automatically takes care of over-identification, and ignores error covariance information that would bias the estimates (Judge et al. 1988, 646). All the coefficients are significant for the petition model, and only one is insignificant (USISFTA) for the employees' model. The R^2 for the production model is excellent. For the certification model it is about three-fourths. For the denial model, it is slightly below 50 per cent, as all its predictors are binary variables for trade agreements.

The income (PDI) and import price (Pm) elasticities are high by traditional demand analysis standards. The income elasticity ranges from 3.42 to 3.94, and the price elasticity from –6.40 to –5.26. The price hypothesis corroborates the argument that if imports were to price themselves out of the United States market, the Office of Trade Adjustment Assistance would be less inclined to certify petitions from firms and employees. A counter-argument might be that the reduction of tariffs occasioned by non-NAFTA countries or even by a Most Favored Nations (MFN) clause can add up to substantial profits, easing pressure to push up the price of imports. Along the same lines, a price rise would be an obstacle to import penetration, and even to transshipment activities for non-

Table 3.2 3SLS system equation results for petitions and employees, 1980–1998

Independent variables	Petitions			Employees		
	Equation 1: Log of certified	Equation 2: Log of denials	Equation 3: Log of values	Equation 1: Log of certified	Equation 2: Log of denials	Equation 3: Log of values
Constant	-44.62 (-8.49)***	2.25 (5.33)***	6.79 (44.44)***	-36.13 (-5.26)***	7.10 (23.91)***	6.79 (45.14)***
LPDI	3.94 (8.01)***			3.42 (5.16)***		
Lpm	-7.55 (-5.20)***			-5.26 (-2.62)***		
Impdum	-0.85 (-3.05)***			-0.93 (-2.32)**		
LCLOSING	1.11 (6.68)***			0.93 (4.10)***		
NAFTA		-1.57 (-2.01)**			-1.06 (-1.95)**	
OMA		1.43 (1.98)**			1.45 (2.49)***	
USISFTA		-1.36 (-2.13)**			-1.26 (-2.91)***	
USCAFTA		1.14 (1.99)**			0.21 (0.57)	
LLABOR			0.28 (6.93)***			0.29 (7.12)***
LCAPITAL			0.10 (3.00)***			0.09 (2.76)**
R^2	0.77	0.31	0.94	0.68	0.48	0.94
DW.	2.15	2.30	1.63	1.65	2.31	1.57

Note: *** = .01, ** = .05, and * = .10 significance levels. Items in parentheses are t-values.

NAFTA countries that try to circumvent the rules of origin in Article 401 of the NAFTA agreement.[4]

The sample period for the United States represents low inflation and substantial growth, translating to high levels of personal disposable income. An earlier study found that the income variable "… seems to have captured the effect of other variables that have contributed to the upsurge in imports" and found import-income elasticities to be in the even larger range of –5.2 to 6.6 (Szenberg et al. 1977, 68). A later study puts income to imports-income elasticities in the range of 3.22 to 3.65 (Lee and Szenberg 1988, 103) which overlaps with our 3.42 to 3.94 certified-income elasticity. The slightly upward drift in the latter estimates can be explained partly by high incomes and less inflation, partly by various trade liberalization policies in our sample period (which decreased the denial of petitions for TAA, thus translating to more certifications), and partly by the fact that our certified-income elasticity is an indirect estimate for the import-income elasticity. This is based on the premise that a strong (almost 1:1) correspondence exists between imports and certification in the sample period. Our estimate corroborates the hypothesis that high income supports high levels of imports, which tend to displace domestic firms and workers, thus enhancing TAA certifications.

The explanation of denials by trade agreement variables yields coefficients that are close to one, indicating a more than proportional effect on denials because of the exponential nature of the model. In another study, OMA had the smaller effect of –0.22 on imports (Lee and Szenberg 1988, 103), equivalent to a 1.25 effect.[5] That study also found an insignificant influence of OMA when it was commingled with other variables. The level of OMA's performance in this model is improved, which might have some expectational effects, since 1981 was the year of its expiration, followed by a surge in imports.

Regarding productivity, the sum coefficient of the production function is less than one, indicating decreasing returns to scale. The results yield the highest R^2 in the model. While it could be improved slightly by using translogs, the full specification of such a function would require a larger sample size to avoid singularity. The contribution of labor clearly dominates, underscoring labor intensiveness in the footwear industry.

---

[4]   The rules of origin in the NAFTA agreement parallel the substantial transformation of the United States custom laws that require members to prove that substantial components and materials of a commodity originate from a member country.

[5]   The binary variables indicate the percentage change in denials if agreement is present, i.e., takes on a value of one. For example, the –1.57 effect of NAFTA on petition denial is $e^{-1.56} = .2$.

Regional Implications

The data permits a test for regional differences in the number of employees affected. For this purpose a regression analysis of the data was done using a complete set of dummy independent variables for five regions – South (S), North East (NE), Mid Atlantic (MA), Midwest (MW), and the West (W). The sample size is 256 for applications denied and 599 for applications certified, clustered by regions for the various years between 1980 and 1998. The two equations below depict the results:

$$\text{Lempcert} = 4.2S + 3.6NE + 3.7MA + 3.9MW + 4.1W \quad \text{D.W} = 2.0 \quad \text{Eq. 4}$$
$$(38.7)\ (32.0)\ (28.0)\ (33.3)\ (7.8) \qquad R^2 = .03$$
$$\text{Lempdeni} = 3.4S + 3.2NE + 3.1MA + 3.8MW - 1.6W \quad \text{D.W} = 2.0 \quad \text{Eq. 5}$$
$$(21.2)\ (22.1)\ (13.5)\ (20.6)\ (-1.2) \qquad R^2 = .04$$

The numbers in parentheses are estimated t-values. The only insignificant result in Eq. 5 is in the West because the number of denied applications in that cell is too small. Except for that one instance, the results are highly significant at the 99 per cent confidence level, and the Durbin-Watson statistic indicates no serial correlation when the observations by regions were kept sequential over the years. For the significant results, the overall finding is that no two regions have the same influence on employment certification. With regard to denials, the same conclusion is reached only without the West region. The fact that the coefficients for the South and Northeast, for instance, are not equal was also verified through a Wald Test for coefficient restrictions. The test was performed for 10 combinations of the five regions. All results for the certified equations turned out significant. Results for the denials are listed below, because they illustrate the case in which the West region is not significant. In the table, C refers to coefficients and the numbers correspond to the order of the coefficients in Eq. 5. The Wald Test for the null hypothesis that the influence of the South and Northeast are the same (C1+C2=0) on denials has a low p-value, indicating that we should reject the null hypothesis that they are equal. It supports the "regional bias hypothesis" that Szenberg et al., found earlier.

		C2	C3	C4	C5
C1:	$x^2 =$	935.43	540.15	866.95	1.61
	Pr. =	(0.00)	(0.00)	(0.00)	(0.00)
	C2		541.94	891.45	1.30
			(0.00)	(0.00)	(0.26)
	C3			551.22	1.11
				(0.00)	(0.29)
	C4				2.56

Consumer Surplus Calculations

The effects of tariffs and trade liberalization are measured by the concept of rent surplus to the various economic agents. Consumer theory predicts that the imposition of a tariff on a free trade economy will contract consumer surplus, expand producer surplus, and after deducting gains to the government, yield a deadweight loss to society. On the other hand, a decrease in tariffs for the footwear industry in particular, assuming imperfect substitutability between domestic and foreign brands, would result in a more-than-proportional gain in consumer surplus. The logic is that a decrease in tariffs causes an initial decrease in the domestic selling price of imports and a switch to imports, creating a consumer surplus. However, domestic prices and thus domestic supply will fall, increasing domestic prices in the constant cost shoe industry in the long run. For our sample period, all of this is going on sequentially; expiration of OMA, the superimposition of NAFTA on USISFTA and USCAFTA, and the accommodating effects of TAA.

TAA enters into the picture via the consumer and welfare maximization problem.[6] In a comparative static framework, as imports impact domestic manufacturers, workers shift to a lower budget line. However, to the extent that they become TAA certified, their budget line will shift back in that proportion, though not necessarily by the full extent of the drop. TAA, therefore, has the potential to benefit both the individual and society. Rather than isolating these effects, we focus on their net estimates as revealed in the related parameters.

The most powerful presence in the sample period is NAFTA, whose trade liberating effects on the footwear industry will be diffused over 10–15 years, with rubber on the high end and non-rubber on the low end. NAFTA countries are not the biggest exporters of footwear to the United States and the rules of origin prevent transshipment of footwear via the NAFTA partners. Meanwhile, the tariff rates for footwear are maintained at a level that is several times the average of other manufactured goods. The empirical evidence indicates that the tariff levels in the footwear industry have fallen somewhat between the immediate pre-NAFTA period and the current period. Using information from the Harmonized Tariff Schedule (HTS), we estimate that the general rates of duty for all classifications under subchapters 6401–6406 average 19.36 per cent in 1990 (the median is 12.5 per cent). By the end of 1993 when the United States was poised to enter the NAFTA agreement, the average was 18.3 per cent (10.5 per cent median). It then hovered around that level annually until 1997.

---

[6]   Broadly speaking, the framework relevant for this analysis is the maximization of a social welfare function such as Welfare = w(Certified $_{t+1}$, Denials$_{t+1}$) subject to the specific estimates for the equation above where Certified = c(*), Denials = d(*), and Values = v(*). Such a model will require the specification of the welfare function, and both exogenous and endogenous values of variables for the model beforehand.

Table 3.3   Parameters for welfare effects

Independent variable	Qm	Qm	Qm
Constant	20	22.86	19.36
	(4.23)***	(4.53)***	(2.82)***
Y	–0.96	–1.13	–0.90
	(2.92)***	(–3.26)***	(–1.90)*
Pm			
Pm/Pd	–0.815	–0.90	–0.80
	(–4.52)***	(–4.525)***	(–2.96)***
OMA	–0.20	–0.22	–0.19
	(–3.50)***	(–4.19)***	(–3.17)***
USISFTA	0.05	0.05	0.05
	(0.78)	(0.75)	(0.65)
USCAFTA	0.08	0.11	0.06
	(1.02)	(1.43)	(0.64)
NAFTA	0.07	0.08	0.05
	(1.46)	(1.73)	(0.81)
CETAA		–0.02	
		(–1.72)	
DETAA		–0.01	
		(–0.86)	
CEPIT		–0.02	
		(–0.73)	
DEPIT		–0.02	
		(–0.98)	
R²	0.99	0.99	0.99
DW	2.13	2.31	2.0
Eq. no.	1	2	3

Note: CETAA is certified employees and DETAA is denied employees. CEPIT and DEPIT are certified and denied petitions. All variables except the dummies are in log form. For significance levels see previous tables. Items in parentheses are t-values.

Table 3.3 shows our estimates for the price elasticity of demand for imports. In Eq. 1, the estimate is –0.815. Eqs. 2 and 3, formulated for sensitivity and robustness checks, demonstrate that the effects of TAA variables (petitions from firms and employees in the form of denials and certifications) change the elasticity from –0.80 to –0.90. However, as the added variables are insignificant, the slight perturbation might be due to a fluke. We therefore use the estimate of Eq. 1 in conjunction with the tariff rates above to estimate consumer surplus due to trade liberalization. The estimates for the expanded consumer surplus for 1990, 1994, and 1997, are $85.11m, $79.33m, and $71.16m, respectively.[7] The average for the 1994–1997 period is estimated at $75.25 million. This is the effect of the removal of deadweight loss to consumers from trade liberalization. Then the cost incurred due to labor displacement is netted out from the benefits.

As a measure of the number of workers displaced due to trade liberalization in the sample period, we used the number of employees applying for TAA in 1994 (3,319) and 1997 (4,713). The Footwear Industries of America (FIA) estimated in August 1998 that total employment in the shoe industry decreased from 62,100 in 1993 to 57,600 in 1994, and from 44,400 in 1997 to 40,500 in 1998. The net declines of 4,500 in 1994 and 4,100 in 1997 are about 1,181 above and 613 below our estimates for 1994 and 1997, respectively. Because the direction of the bias is both positive and negative, we make no adjustment. Besides, the split between numbers certified and denied in the TAA estimates compels us to use the TAA estimates. Using those estimates, the first part of Table 3.5 develops cost estimates of the net labor cost. Gross labor costs without TAA benefits are estimated at $60.96 million and $97.71 million for 1994 and 1997, respectively. The labor cost with TAA benefits is estimated at $38.31 million and $67.28 million for 1994 and 1997. The net labor cost for the two years are $22.64 million in 1994 and $30.43 million in 1997.

Table 3.4   Costs and benefits in footwear

	PV	Benefits	PV	Costs	Net benefits	
Time	1994	1997	1994	1997	1994	1997
Value:	79.33	71.16	22.64	30.43	56.69	40.73
Present value from $PV = \frac{1}{2}(t^2)0_m V_m (1+d)^i$:						
1	77.48	69.51	22.12	29.72	55.37	39.79
2	75.68	67.89	21.60	29.03	54.08	38.86
3	73.92	66.31	21.10	28.35	52.82	37.96
4	72.20	64.77	20.61	27.69	51.59	37.07
5	70.52	63.26	20.13	27.05	50.39	36.21
Total present value in perpetuity: $PV = 1/r$:						
Total:	3,329	2,986	950	1,277	2,036	1,881

We now have static, no growth without discounting, estimates of costs and benefits for the endpoints of our sample period, reflecting the benefits of trade liberalization and TAA. Assuming that the United States economy was at its potential level of growth, g = 4 per cent to reflect combined labor force and productivity growth, and a discount factor equivalent to the five-year Treasury

---

[7]   The equation used is $\frac{1}{2}(t^2)0_m V_m$, where t is the tariff rates, 0_m is the price elasticity of imports estimated at .81 (Eq. 1, Table 3), and V_m is the value of imports, viz., $5570m, $5813m, and $5390m, for 1990, 1994, 1997, respectively.

Bill rate (approximately r = 6.33 per cent between 1994–1997) we can now get a net benefit calculation for a five-year period and in perpetuity. Table 3.4 places the benefits and costs from Table 3.5 in the first row, followed by the discounted values with d = g – r, t = tariff, and Vm = value of imports. Trade liberalization confers consumer surplus to the extent of $3,329 million in 1994 and $2,986 million in 1997. The corresponding labor displacement costs are $950 million and $1,277 million, yielding benefits of $2,036 million and $1,881 million for the respective years.

The second part of Table 3.5 cross checks the Department of Labor standard ratio that 20,000 jobs are gained for a $1 billion increase in trade. It does so in its modus tollen form, viz., $1 billion lost to domestic sales due to import competition yields 20,000 in job losses. In the process, we used the median decline in tariffs computed from HTS tables, an exchange rate based on price differentials, and the unit value for price estimates. The bottom line indicates that the Department of Labor ratio yields 3,150 jobs affected in 1994 and 4,027 in 1997. The department's ratio yields a forecast error of 169 (3,319 TAA applicants less 3,150) in 1994, which is a fair rule-of-thumb forecast. The forecast error in 1997 is wider, viz., 686 (4,713 less 4,027), but as we shall show in the simulation section, it does not mean that the rule-of-thumb is invalidated.

Simulating Welfare Benefits

The positive benefits we credited to TAA are conditioned on the assumptions of many critical ratios. In particular, we have used estimates of import elasticities, tariff rates, months in job searching, years left for displaced workers to retire, per cent of the displaced that are permanently unemployed, and exchange rate assumptions between foreign and imported shoes as factors in our estimates. In this section, we subject those ratios to some perturbations in order to get a sense of the robustness of our estimates. We begin with the estimate we used for the number of displaced workers in the cost analysis of Table 3.5. We focus on whether the assumption of 20,000 jobs lost per $1 billion in trade gains, as estimated by the Department of Labor (DOL) validate the criticisms the DOL has received in the literature.

In our estimates of the sample size of displaced workers, we assume that the import elasticity is 0.815, and an exchange ratio of 3.2 foreign to domestic pairs of shoes prevails. A cross check in Table 3.3 indicates that the ratio could be in the –0.80 to –0.90 band, but that the confidence level of that band is questionable. It was therefore decided to simulate the true ratio for 1997, using a normal distribution with a mean of 0.815 and standard deviation of 0.05; i.e., $N \sim (0.085, 0.05)$. Similarly, we have referred to the 1988 Lee and Szenberg estimate of the exchange ratio of 2:1, which made us specify a uniform distribution for the exchange ratio of $U \sim (2.0, 3.2)$. The result of the simulation using the methodology of Part 2 of Table 3.5 on the mean value yields 4,969 displaced workers, exceeding

Table 3.5   Estimates of losses due to NAFTA

PV of losses	1994	1997	Reference	Source
Part 1: Cost estimates:				
Displaced workers:	3319	4713	T	Office of TAA
Denied:	339	77		ibid.,
Certified:	980	4636	Z	ibid.,
Assumptions:				
Hourly wage:	$7.80	$8.49	A	FIA: Shoestat
Average weekly hours:	37.40	37.20	B	FIA: Shoestat
Yearly earnings:	$14,547.00	$16,423.00	C	C=AxB
Weeks remained unhired:	18.20	18.20	D	Lee and Szenberg
Per cent permanently unemployed	25.7%	25.7%	E	ibid.,
Years left for retirement:	3.9	3.9	F	ibid.,
Total loss for certified and denied:				
Number permanently displaced:	853	1,211		G=TxE
Income lost for 3.9 years ($M):	$48.39	$77. 58		H=(FxGxC)/$1M
No. unemp. for 18.2 /52 years:	863	1,226		I=.743Tx.35years
Income lost for 18.2/52 years:	$12.56	$20.13		J=IxC/$1m
Total loss without TAA:	$60.95M	$97.71M		H+J
Assistance provided by TAA:				
No. certified displaced permanently:	766	1,192		K=ZxE
Income received for 3.9 years ($M):	$30.42	$53.42		3.9Kx.7C
No. remain unemp. for18.2/52 years:	775	1,205.59		L=0.743Z*.35
Income lost for 18.2/52 years($M):	$7.89	$13.86		M=L*.7C/$1M
Total benefits via TAA:	$38.31M	$67.28M		
Net labor cost:	$22.64M	$30.43M		
Part 2: Crosscheck displaced:				
Elasticity of demand for imports:	(0.815)	(0.815)	a	Table 3.4
Assume: Fall in tariff equals increase sales:	2%	2%	b	Median drop.
Then: Factor for increase in imports:	1.64%	1.64%	c	axb
Million pairs (MP) of imports:	1101	1213	d	FIA Shoestat
Increase in demand for imports: (MP)	18.06	19.89	e	dx(c/100)
Ratio of domestic to import price:	29:9	32:10	f	Lee and Szenberg
3.2 Import = 1 domestic shoes:	5.64	6.22		e/f
Price per domestic pair:	$27.92	$32.39	g	Unit value
Fall in domestic sales:	$157M	$201M	h	fxg
20,000 jobs per $1billion:	3,151	4,027		Census ratio

the total applicants for TAA benefits in 1977 by 256. The range of estimated displaced workers is between 4,027 in Table 3.5 and 4,969 from the simulation, which includes the 4,713 TAA applicants. As the range was premised on the critical Department of Labor assumption, the above analysis supports its validation in this analysis.

Along the same lines, we have simulated the costs and benefits to consumers for 1997. For 1,000 replications, a normal distribution with mean values of Table 3.5, and a .05 standard deviation for time spent in job search, time left for retirement (in years), and percentage of workers permanently displaced, yielded a net job loss after deducting TAA benefits of $30.74 million in line with Table 3.5. The simulation of consumer surplus estimates used the simulated import elasticity in the displaced workers sample value and the median decrease in the tariff rates of 2 per cent around a stable 18 per cent average in the NAFTA years. The benefits were simulated at $71.36 million, slightly above the $71.16 million estimate in Table 3.4. Therefore, the net benefit in 1997 is $40.62 million, only slightly less than the $40.73 million figure in Table 3.4, clearly indicating some robustness in the estimates.

Conclusion

We have presented several measures of TAA performance in the United States economy during the NAFTA and other trade liberalization agreements. With the availability of time series data on TAA's performance, we were able to explain its certification and denial processes with traditional trade and policy variables successfully. About 50 per cent of the policy measures explaining why affected employees and petitions are denied benefits are explained by binary variables that capture the presence of those regulations, given the rate of certification and production activities. Nearly 80 per cent of the certifications are attributable to plant closings, import surges, import prices, and personal disposable income. The strength of United States productivity has empowered the nation to carry out TAA policies.

On the welfare side, we have demonstrated that the positive net benefits from the early stage of liberalization would not be possible but for TAA's assistance in the sample period. The simulation model indicates some stability in the estimates, and lends some credence to the Department of Labor job gains statement. In the longer term, when tariffs will be eliminated over 10 to 15 years for NAFTA, and threats of sanctions are played out, it will be necessary to redo the analysis with longer time series. A more general equilibrium point of view, extending the analysis of TAA's participation to other industries, and taking Mexico, Canada, and the rest of the world into account explicitly, would be needed to decide the value of TAA's overall performance. As of now, the partial equilibrium analysis undertaken here, taking the open economy into account implicitly, supports the trade liberalization paradigm and the enhancement of consumer surplus.

Chapter 4

The Garment Industry

Introduction

This study recognizes that the literature has documented the severe impacts of trade liberalization on the garment industry. Traditionally, the United States garment industry has been characterized by low or insignificant concentration. It is a labor-intensive, slow-growth, protected industry with a high proportion of unskilled workers. It has been a traditional price- and expenditure-sensitive industry, i.e., people will tend to buy less clothing in proportion to increases in prices and expenditures.

This industry has been challenged during the 1970s, 1980s, and 1990s by regulatory changes, new technology, and globalization. The emergence of newly industrialized countries contributed to the decline in employment in the industry. However, after the 1975 recession, exports of textiles and apparel doubled, and shipments grew by about 24 per cent, primarily due to industry restructuring that enhanced productivity and international competitiveness, and the impetus from the Multifiber Arrangement (MFA). However, the 1980s saw a counter-cyclical effect. Import surges correlated strongly with the high value of the dollar, and with some loopholes in the MFA, which did not restrain the imports of a majority of product categories. By the end of the 1980s, the trade balance in textile and apparel improved with the OECD countries, but remained off-balance with the Big Four (China, Taiwan, Hong Kong, and South Korea) where the dollar remained strong.

Compared with the 1970s and 1980s, the surge in imports in the 1990s was meteoric. The early 1990s saw an exit of inefficient companies, somewhat increasing the concentration. This was sped by the "Quick Response" program of larger firms that linked manufacturers with suppliers and retailers.[1] The industry's outlook became dismal and the industry continues to decline to date[2]

---

[1] Quick Response was a cost cutting effort that lowered inventory, used frequent markdowns, and shortened reordering cycles. Also, it called for extensive capital modernization efforts, which the smaller and medium size firms could least afford (*US Industrial Outlook* 1990, 35–93).

[2] Basic differences exist in the modeling of the Uruguay Round and NAFTA. A common motive is to integrate the developing country into the global economy via trade liberalization. But NAFTA's domain of operation is restricted to trade between Mexico, Canada, and the US, while the Uruguay Round's domain of influence is more global.

in the presence of trade liberalization in 1994 when the Uruguay Round became finalized and the NAFTA agreements became effective. The major premise for the bleak outlook was that United States wages relative to productivity put the domestic textile and apparel producers at a competitive disadvantage to foreign counterparts, resulting in a steady decline in employment. Meanwhile, the share of traditional international competitors has been changing. In particular, the largest companies were losing shares to Mexico and the Caribbean.[3]

The purpose of this chapter is to show that the concurrent increase in the certification of TAA benefits and decline in the domestic industry have had a positive balancing effect, arresting the industry's state of decline. In particular, we will show that income benefits from TAA adjustments resulted in a net positive welfare gain for the United States industry, in effect, validating the expected positive effect of trade liberalization with TAA accommodating policies for the industry. The remainder of this paper includes a discussion of the model of TAA data, an estimation of welfare benefits, and conclusions.

Costs and Benefits Specifications and Analysis of Trade Liberalization

This section measures the cost of liberalization based on the impact of imports. A measure of such a cost is directly related to the number of displaced employees. To the extent that the displaced workers are certified for trade adjustment benefits, we can measure this direct cost. However, the TAA benefits are a relief of some of the cost burden, which reduces the actual cost. In the next sections we consider the welfare effect of liberalization and then provide a reconciliation of Computational General Equilibrium estimate of benefits from the liberalization of the economy.

Measuring the Cost of Liberalization

Table 4.1 erects some milestones, showing paradigmatic shifts in qualifying trends. The estimates suggest that a paradigmatic shift has occurred in the new versus old forms of TAA. While the purpose of TAA remained essentially the same since its introduction in 1962, that is, to compensate workers for import displacement costs, and to enhance occupational and geographical mobility, only an unintended small number of workers qualified under the strict laws of the Trade Expansion Act. Later, in 1974, when the Act came under The Labor Department's jurisdiction, its labor performance improved and continued in that

---

[3]   Between 1992–1997, Mexico's share of United States imports (SIC 23) doubled, from 6 to 12.5 per cent, while Taiwan's share fell from 7.8 to 4.6 per cent; Hong Kong's, from 13.4 to 8 per cent, and China's from 16.8 to 15.9 per cent (*US Industrial Outlook* 1994 and 1999).

direction during the liberalization eras of the 1980s and 1990s. The 1994–1998 NAFTA liberalization era clearly witnessed increased trends in both petitions and employees certified for TAA benefits for the industry. Denials averaged only about 2 per cent for both petitions and employees after NAFTA, down from about 7 per cent during the 1980–1993 period. Table 4.1 also shows similar reactions for certification for the Free Trade Agreements of Canada and Israel. However, the FTA agreements were not always followed by a lower denial percentage. For instance, after the USISFTA, the percentage of employees denied TAA increased from 11 to 17 per cent for the 1987–1999 period and the number of denials for petitions stayed at about 12 per cent after the USCAFTA period of 1985–1999. The NAFTA period is, therefore, unique for demonstrating that percentages of petitions and employees certified and denied reacted inversely.

Table 4.1a Petitions and employment experience in the garment industry, 1980–1999

Various years	Petitions				Employees			
	Total certified	Total denied	Annual % certified	Annual % denied	Total certified	Total denied	Annual % certified	Annual % denied
1980–99:	3,791	1,783			355,471	110,076		
Data for NAFTA comparison:								
1980–93	2,034	1,633	4.13%	7.04%	168,072	100,040	3.64%	6.99%
1994–99	1,757	150	9.27%	1.68%	187,419	10,036	10.54.%	1.82%
Data for USISFTA comparison:								
1980–86	955	1,200	4.20%	11.22%	53,839	72,770	0.52%	11.02%
1987–99	2,836	583	6.23%	2.72%	301,652	37,306	42.43%	16.94%
Data for USCAFTA comparison:								
1980–84	577	925	3.81%	12.97%	35,565	62,556	2.50%	14.21%
1985–99	3,214	858	21.19%	12.03%	319,926	47,520	6.42%	3.08%

Source: Estimated by the authors from data provided by the Office of Trade Adjustment Assistance

Definition of constants and variables apparel and textile industry

CERTIFIED = number of petitions/employees certified for TAA.
DENIALS = number of petitions/employees denied TAA.
PDI = personal disposable income in constant 1982-84 dollars.
Pm = import price in unit value.
Impdum = a dummy of one for years in which import increases.
CLOSING = plant closing.

NAFTA = a dummy of one for NAFTA 1994 onwards (Passed: November 1993.)

OMA = a dummy of one for 1977–1981 for the OMA years (Expired: 1981).

USISFTA = a dummy of one for 1985 onwards for the United States & Israel Free Trade Agreement.

USCAFTA = a dummy of one for 1988 onwards for the United States & Canada Free Trade Agreement.

L = log-arithmetic values.

Table 4.1b   four firms concentration ratios, apparel and textile industry

SIC	Description	1958	1972	1992
2311	Men's and boy's suits and coats	13	19	39
2321	Men's and boy's shirts and nightwear	16	20	28
2327	Men's and boy's separate trousers	11	25	
2328	Men's and boy's work clothing	15	40	
2329	Men's and boy's clothing	14	17	18
2331	Women' s and misses' blouses and waists	11	10	12
2335	Women's and misses' dresses	4	9	11
2337	Women's and misses' suits and coats	3	7	24
2339	Women's and misses' outwear	10	14	12
2341	Women's and children's underwear	8	14	29
2342	Brassieres and allied garments	28	35	56
2352	Hats and caps, except millinery	29	25	
2361	Children's dresses and blouses	13	14	18
2363	Children's coats and suits	4	17	
2369	Children's outerwear	13[1]	16	26
2381	Fabric dress and work gloves	30	42	64
2385	Waterproof outergarments		31	64
2387	Apparel belts	19	22	33
2392	Housefurnishings			39
2395	Pleating and stitching	3[1]	19	19
2396	Automotive and apparel trimmings	58	70	29

Source: Up to 1972: 1972 Census of Manufactures, US Department of Commerce (MC72 (SR)-2; 1992: Census of Manufactures. 1 is for 1963. Definitional changes of the apparel and textile industry categories after 1992, make it impossible to compare the ratios to the recent censuses.

Table 4.2 gives our estimates of the costs of total displacement to the garment industry. A measure of the total displaced workers is the number of persons applying for TAA benefits for the years 1980 to 1998, which is, in effect, the total number of persons certified plus the total number of persons denied TAA benefits. In order to make a credible estimate, we also had to rely on several generally available parameters from the literature. One such variable is the length of time it takes for job searches after displacement. The USITC (May 1999, 30) study estimates that the percentage of textile and apparel workers who found new jobs within five years was 90.6 per cent and 86.4 per cent, respectively. Also, the average duration of unemployment rates was 2.1 and 2.3 quarters, respectively. For the apparel workers, 2.3 quarters is 6.9 months or 27.6 weeks; the analogous number for the textile workers is 25.2 weeks, making the average for both about 26.4 weeks (Column 6). The percentage of persons permanently unemployed (Column 7) is also from the USITC study, reflecting average re-employed displaced persons over a five-year period of 86.4 per cent in the apparel industry, and 90.6 in the textile industry over a five-year period. Finally, the imputation of (Column 8) an estimated time of 3.9 years remaining for retirement of the displaced workers is taken from Lee and Szenberg (1988).

Table 4.3 indicates our estimate of TAA benefits that must be balanced against the cost estimate of Table 4.2. The columns are sequential to those of Table 4.2, as they proceed to display gross potential gains due to TAA benefits accruing to a displaced worker, and afterwards to be netted from labor cost. Column 18 of Table 4.3 indicates that the benefits levels were particularly enhanced during the NAFTA period, increasing from $453 million in 1995 to $702 million in 1998. As a result, the benefits-to-cost ratio was particularly high for that period, with a mode of 67 per cent.

The 67 per cent estimate of TAA benefits to displaced garment workers is most likely conservative. A first approximation of its downward bias would include some of the crucial inputs discussed in the model section including other compensations. A $500 maximum job search allowance available to displaced workers was added to the package. Also, we can add a measure of relocation and reimbursement for reasonable and necessary expenses. We have made an approximate estimate of this in Table 4.4. Added together, the estimate falls short of one million. If we increase it by a million dollars, then the TAA benefits estimate would not significantly increase the 67 per cent benefits to cost ratio. In other words, about three-fourths of the workers' costs are compensated by the TAA during the NAFTA era.

Estimates of Welfare Benefits to the Economy Due to Trade Liberalization

The theoretical literature has clearly established the benefits of trade liberalization to the economy. At least three propositions are offered as to why quota and tariff elimination enhances welfare. Assuming substitutability of excess demand between the taxed and all other goods, one proposition assumes that some goods have the highest tariff rate, and a reduction of that rate, not necessarily an elimination of

Table 4.2   Estimates of losses due to import impact, 1980–1998

Year	(1+2) Displaced workers	1 Total certified TAA	2 Total denied TAA	3 Wage rate	4 Average weekly hours	5 Annual income (3*4)*52	6 Weeks not hired	7 Percent perm. unemp.	8 Years to retire	9 (2*7) # perm. displaced	10 (5*8*9)/1M Inc. loss to retire.	11 2*(88.5)*(26.4/52) # unemp. 26/52 yrs	12 (11*5)/1M Inc. loss: 26/52 yrs	13 (12+10) Total loss w/o TAA
1980	34095	19765	14330	7.27	39.70	$15,008	26.4	0.115	3.9	3920.93	$229.50	15319.15	$229.91	$459.41
1981	28823	5825	22998	7.99	39.80	$16,536	26.4	0.115	3.9	3314.65	$213.76	12950.40	$214.15	$427.91
1982	24547	5213	19334	8.49	38.90	$17,174	26.4	0.115	3.9	2822.91	$189.07	11029.16	$189.41	$378.48
1983	6652	3011	3641	8.83	40.10	$18,412	26.4	0.115	3.9	764.98	$54.93	2988.79	$55.03	$109.96
1984	4004	1751	2253	9.19	40.70	$19,450	26.4	0.115	3.9	460.46	$34.93	1799.03	$34.99	$69.92
1985	10273	6561	3712	9.54	40.50	$20,091	26.4	0.115	3.9	1181.40	$92.57	4615.74	$92.74	$185.31
1986	18215	11713	6502	9.73	40.70	$20,593	26.4	0.115	3.9	2094.73	$168.23	8184.14	$168.53	$336.76
1987	17245	13074	4171	9.91	41.00	$21,128	26.4	0.115	3.9	1983.18	$163.41	7748.31	$163.71	$327.12
1988	15408	12585	2823	10.19	41.10	$21,778	26.4	0.115	3.9	1771.92	$150.50	6922.93	$150.77	$301.27
1989	16014	12946	3068	10.48	41.00	$22,343	26.4	0.115	3.9	1841.61	$160.48	7195.21	$160.77	$321.24
1990	33940	27413	6527	10.83	40.80	$22,977	26.4	0.115	3.9	3903.10	$349.76	15249.50	$350.39	$700.14
1991	25019	19214	5805	11.18	40.70	$23,661	26.4	0.115	3.9	2877.19	$265.50	11241.23	$265.98	$531.49
1992	16547	14583	1964	11.46	41.00	$24,433	26.4	0.115	3.9	1902.91	$181.32	7434.69	$181.65	$362.97
1993	17330	14418	2912	11.74	41.40	$25,274	26.4	0.115	3.9	1992.95	$196.44	7786.50	$196.80	$393.24
1994	29801	27351	2450	12.07	42.00	$26,361	26.4	0.115	3.9	3427.12	$352.33	13389.82	$352.97	$705.30
1995	31363	29826	1537	12.37	41.60	$26,759	26.4	0.115	3.9	3606.75	$376.40	14091.64	$377.08	$753.47
1996	48126	46120	2006	12.77	41.60	$27,624	26.4	0.115	3.9	5534.49	$596.25	21623.38	$597.33	$1,193.58
1997	45287	43459	1828	13.17	42.00	$28,763	26.4	0.115	3.9	5208.01	$584.22	20347.80	$585.27	$1,169.49
1998	37598	35558	2040	14.49	41.70	$31,420	26.4	0.115	3.9	4323.77	$529.83	16893.07	$530.78	$1060.61

Table 4.3   Estimates of TAA benefits received due to import impact on the garment industry, 1980–1998

Years	13 (12+10) Total loss w/o TAA	14 1*7: # Cert. and displaced permanently	15 (8*14) *.7*5)/1M years	16 1*(1−col8)*(col 8/52) #unemployed for col. 8/52 yrs	17 16*.7*Col 5/1m Income loss for col. 8/52 yrs	18 15+17 Total TAA benefits	19 13−18 Net labour cost	20 18/13 TAA to losses
1980	$459.41	2272.98	93.13	8880.57	93.30	186.43	272.99	0.41
1981	$427.91	669.88	30.24	2617.22	30.30	60.54	367.38	0.14
1982	$378.48	599.50	28.11	2342.24	28.16	56.26	322.22	0.15
1983	$109.96	346.27	17.41	1352.87	17.44	34.84	75.12	0.32
1984	$69.92	201.37	10.69	786.74	10.71	21.40	48.51	0.31
1985	$185.31	754.52	41.38	2947.91	41.46	82.84	102.46	0.45
1986	$336.76	1347.00	75.72	5262.74	75.86	151.59	185.18	0.45
1987	$327.12	1503.51	86.72	5874.25	86.88	173.60	153.52	0.53
1988	$301.27	1447.28	86.05	5654.54	86.20	172.25	129.02	0.57
1989	$321.24	1488.79	90.81	5816.74	90.98	181.79	139.45	0.57
1990	$700.14	3152.50	197.75	12316.87	198.10	395.85	304.29	0.57
1991	$531.49	2209.61	142.73	8633.00	142.99	285.72	245.77	0.54
1992	$362.97	1677.05	111.86	6552.25	112.06	223.92	139.05	0.62
1993	$393.24	1658.07	114.40	6478.12	114.61	229.01	164.22	0.58
1994	$705.30	3145.37	226.36	12289.01	226.76	453.12	252.18	0.64
1995	$753.47	3429.99	250.57	13401.05	251.02	501.58	251.89	0.67
1996	$1,193.58	5303.80	399.98	20722.07	400.70	800.68	392.90	0.67
1997	$1,169.49	4997.79	392.44	19526.46	393.15	785.60	383.89	0.67
1998	$1,060.61	4089.17	350.76	15976.48	351.39	702.14	358.47	0.66

it, would improve welfare. Another proposition, based on the same assumption, argues that if the highest tariff rate cannot be reduced, and a tariff is imposed on a subset of freely traded goods, then welfare will be improved to a degree. A third proposition drops the substitutability assumption, and argues that a proportionate elimination of all tariffs would improve welfare (Bhagwati et al. 1998, ch. 35).

Traditional estimates of benefits from trade liberalization revolve around both the partial (PE) and general equilibrium (GE) viewpoints. On the PE side, the gains appear much smaller. For instance, it was estimated that the gain was around $8.6 billion for 1996 (USITC May 1999, 29). On the GE side, Trela and Whalley (1990, 1190) estimated that the elimination of quotas and tariffs in the textile and apparel sectors by developed countries globally has resulted in a $23 billion gain in 1986 dollars, with approximately $12.3 billion going to the United States. A study by Yang et al., based on the GTAP model using a four-tier experiment, estimated the global gain at $27 billion in 1986 dollars. A more recent GE study by Harrison et al., summarized other studies in the area and estimated much higher global gains under the Uruguay Round in the $96-$171 billion range (in 1992 dollars), projected to the year 2005. Their estimated gain for the United States was $13 billion, using a static model. An updated study for 1996 reported $5.7 billion for just tariff reduction, and $10.4 billion if both tariffs and quotas are removed (USITC May 1999, xv–xvi).

While the estimates of those two views diverge, they both aim at capturing gains of liberalization through the Consumer Surplus (CS) that is generated. The PE model uses the area below a postulated demand curve, the equilibrium price line, and the y-axis as a measure of CS. Its major advantage is its simplicity of estimate based on the area of a triangle. The major disadvantage of the PE model is its inability to incorporate feedback effects in cross-industry and cross-country analysis. The GE models, on the other hand, postulate a welfare or utility index for a representative regional household, which obtains endowment income from the producers. The major disadvantage is its plethora of welfare assumptions, and until recently, the consistent data in which to compare countries. The major premise (Yang et al. 1997, 253) with regards to trade liberalization is that restraints, such as MFA, quantitatively restrict exports of textiles (R) from developing countries, and apply nondiscriminatory tariffs (t) on imports of textile and clothing. Consequently, given R and t, when R is binding, R determines import volume in a rather accounting manner, that is, $p_d = f(DD_d, R) = p_w(1+t)(1+q)$. With liberalization, the problem at hand is the phasing out of export quotas over ten years, and the reduction of tariffs on imported goods.

Suppose the regional excess demand function is $Z^i_p = f$ (Demand –Supply), where $i = 0....n$. Within that GE demand and supply framework, Country A can export to a restricted market or the ROW. If we let those demands be Z^1_p in the restricted market, and Z^2_p respectively, then the sum of those two excess demand curves, or rather the crossing of the demand for imports with supply of exports, would yield the equilibrium price and quantity, P_e and Q_e. In general, if a quota price $P = P_w(1+q) > P_e$, and a world price $P_w < P_e$, then a kinked demand curve

Table 4.4   Relocation expenses, 1996

Description:	Numbers	1996	Source
Part I: 3 × workers average weekly wage:			
Average weekly wage rate	1	$12.77	
Average weekly hours worked	2	41.6	
Average weekly income earned	3	$531.23	#1×#2
Number getting relocation benefits	4	5,304	
Percent of workers relocating	5	0.1	2097/17655= 11.8% (AHS 95)
Number certified and displaced permanently	6	530	
Number getting relocation benefits	7	53	
Beneficiaries × 3 × average weekly earnings	8	$84,526.45	(3×#3)×#7
Part II: 80% of reasonable and necessary expenses:			
House hunting trip:			
Number of house hunters:	9	16	(520/17655)×#12 (owner rate)
Average days house hunting	10	7	
Perdiem at conus rate = $70	11	$7,654.54	#9×#10x rate
Average of 500 miles @ 31 cents	12	$155.00	500×.31
Total house hunting trips	13	$7,809.54	#11+#12
Brokerage fees:			
US average sales price	14	$115,800	US housing market conditions
Selling fees	15	$6,948.00	6%
Buying costs	16	$3,474.00	3%
Movement of HH goods	17	$1,500	
Total housing cost	18	$11,922	#15+#16+#17
Sum of Part II	19	$19,732	#18+#13
Workers reimbursement (80%)	20	$15,785	#19*.8
Sum Parts I and II :	21	$104,257.98	#19+#8

will result. A fall in tariffs would increase the demand for goods and services in the restricted market. This would be indicated by a shift of the demand curve to the right. It means that exporters in the restricted market will get a higher price, say P_c, and the abolishing of quotas would be spread over two components—with and without tariffs. In a static environment, the extent of the gain is a function of the level of tariff or quota elimination, holding saving and investment constant. In the following sections, we present our estimates of these two methodologies.

A Partial Equilibrium Estimate of Benefits from Liberalization to the Economy

We will make two specifications for the purpose of estimating benefits and calculating the impact of TAA benefits. In partial equilibrium (PE) models, tariffs enter directly into the calculation given the equation $\frac{1}{2}(t^2)0_m V_m$, where t is the tariff rate, 0_m is the price elasticity of imports, and V_m is the value of imports. The estimate will vary according to the sources of estimates for the input. Since the equation measures consumer surplus, we will restrict the value of imports to United States imports for consumption, as against United States general imports. A straightforward measure of tariff rates can, therefore, be the actual import charges divided by the United States imports for consumption. The tariff estimates for Mexico and Canada, individually and in combination, are scarcely equal to 1 per cent for our industry group—SIC 23 (see Table 4.5). Also, the USITC tariff grouping of NAFTA countries is within the same range as the top part. The bottom part on the right shows substantially larger tariff rates for the industry in all countries. More detailed levels of aggregation suggest higher tariff rates. In 1996, the USITC shows tariff rates ranging from 2.2 to 13.9 per cent and tariff equivalents ranging from 0.1 to 6 per cent for 15 sectors (USITC 1999, 12). The average rates were 7.66 and 1.4 per cent respectively, combining to about 9.0 per cent for 1996.

The next major input for our PE welfare benefit formula is the elasticity of import. We will adjust elasticity estimates for TAA certification and denial in line with the approach found in Szenberg et al. (1977) and Lee and Szenberg (1988). Essentially, the PE specification for elasticity is a double log arithmetic function of imports on income, relative prices, and other variables. Using the OLS regression equation, we came up with a best elasticity estimate of approximately –0.88, as indicated in Table 4.6. This is the coefficient for the relative prices with and without NAFTA influences when TAA benefits are incorporated. The other equations are attempts to improve upon that estimate including dummy variables for the various time frames identified in Table 4.5. In particular, dummy variables were created for NAFTA, United States-Israel, and United States-Canada free trade areas. Since the latter was overshadowed by NAFTA, it did not yield good results. Also, the United States-Israel FTA dummy conflicted with the constant, being a series of ones, and since the constant was significant, the United States-Israel FTA variable was dropped.

Table 4.5 Tariff rates for SIC 23 apparel and related products

Year	Mexico Import charges	Mexico Value of imports	Mexico Pct.	Canada Import charges	Canada Value of imports	Canada Pct.	Mexico and Canada Import charges	Mexico and Canada Value of imports	Mexico and Canada Pct.
1989	4,262	990,414	0.43%	2,191	338,796	0.65%	6,453.00	1,329,210.00	0.49%
1990	7,541	1,200,514	0.63%	3,106	322,323	0.96%	10,647.00	1,522,837.00	0.70%
1991	11,889	1,487,643	0.80%	4,291	377,740	1.14%	16,180.00	1,865,383.00	0.87%
1992	14,617	1,957,970	0.75%	4,319	492,263	0.88%	18,936.00	2,450,233.00	0.77%
1993	18,079	2,449,127	0.74%	6,101	615,559	0.99%	24,180.00	3,064,686.00	0.79%
1994	22,176	2,876,941	0.77%	7,949	788,106	1.01%	30,125.00	3,665,047.00	0.82%
1995	29,374	3,673,089	0.80%	8,517	986,607	0.86%	37,891.00	4,659,696.00	0.81%
1996	39,061	4,670,307	0.84%	11,534	1,186,149	0.97%	50,595.00	5,856,456.00	0.86%
1997	49,826	6,274,609	0.79%	13,683	1,433,855	0.95%	63,509.00	7,708,464.00	0.82%
1998	58,164	7,687,945	0.76%	16,112	1,702,594	0.95%	74,276.00	9,390,539.00	0.79%
1999	70,395	8,778,148	0.80%	26,322	1,868,759	1.41%	96,717.00	10,646,907.00	0.91%

Year	All countries Import charges	All countries Value of imports	All countries Pct.	For NAFTA for all countries Import charges	For NAFTA for all countries Value of imports	For NAFTA for all countries Pct.
1989	1,518,531.00	25,508,753.00	5.95%			
1990	1,496,274.00	26,746,981.00	5.59%			
1991	1,538,972.00	27,376,664.00	5.62%			
1992	1,747,674.00	32,644,507.00	5.35%			
1993	1,882,629.00	35,474,941.00	5.31%			
1994	1,978,252.00	38,560,817.00	5.13%	17,400.00	2,136,407.00	0.81%
1995	1,921,034.00	41,208,106.00	4.66%	18,354.00	2,500,435.00	0.73%
1996	1,827,538.00	43,074,551.00	4.24%	27,998.00	3,046,006.00	0.92%
1997	1,972,433.00	50,190,456.00	3.93%	35,998.00	4,040,165.00	0.89%
1998	2,076,192.00	55,837,793.00	3.72%	41,521.00	4,769,830.00	0.87%
1999	2,525,545.00	59,114,353.00	4.27%	64,926.00	6,609,784.00	0.98%

Source: USITC: Trade Data Web. Tariff rates are actual import charges divided by the custom value of imports.

Table 4.6   Regression models for import elasticity, 1989–1998

Independent variables:	Dependent variables			
	Qm	Qm	Qm	Qm
Constant	11.43 (5.35)***	11.60 (5.67)***	14.33 (2.12)*	11.4 (1.78)
Y	0.73 (6.23)***	0.73 (6.47)***	0.50 (1.24)	0.57 (1.54)
Pm/Pd	−0.88 (−7.43)***	−0.88 (−7.76)***	−1.14 (−1.93)	−0.56 (−0.82)
NAFTA	−0.04 (−0.83)			−0.37 (−1.38)
CETAA	−0.40 (−7.85)***	−0.43 (−11.99)***		
DETAA	0.16 (4.67)***	0.18 (6.81)***		
CEPIT			−0.39 (−1.82)	−0.003 (−0.01)
DEPIT			0.15 (1.36)	−0.11 (−0.11)
R2	.99	.99	.77	.86
DW	2.58	2.24	1.66	1.75
EQ. No.	1	2	3	4

Note: USITC Trade Web Data. CETAA is certified employees; DETAA denied employees. CEPIT and DEPIT is certified and denied petitions respectively. Pm is import price, Pd is domestic price. All variables except the dummies are in log form. *** = Significant at 99% level; **= Significant at the 95% level, and * = 90 Significant at the 90% level.

We have seen that the tariff rate can take a maximum value of up to 13 per cent for apparel, and averages about 0.9 per cent for the textile and apparel sectors. With the maximum tariff level, an import elasticity measure of –0.88 and the respective values of imports for years 1994 and 1998, we have performed net benefit calculations displayed in Table 4.7. The last column indicates that the net benefits are greatly enhanced in the years following the NAFTA period of 1994. However, as tariffs fall, we should expect lower benefits. How low tariffs will fall depends on other factors, of which we now consider a few. To the extent that a reduction in tariffs reduces wage rates and enhances returns on capital, specialization in the trading countries will improve. While the rate among NAFTA countries can be minimal, it is unlikely that the rate with the rest of the world will be the same.

Assessing biases on the benefit side is not easy. The major source of bias is inherent in the PE estimate itself. The essence of the argument resides with the piggy-backing of consumers' indifference with producers' possibility curves along changing price ratios among trading countries.[4]

Table 4.7 **The time path of the present value. Net benefits of trade liberalization in the garment industry, 1994 vs. 1998**

Time	PV benefits			PV costs		Net benefits	
	1994	1998	Average	1994	1998	1994	1998
Values:	297.30	476.51	386.58	252.18	358.47	45.12	118.04
Present values from the formula: $PV = \frac{1}{2}(t^2)0_m V_m(1+d)^i$							
1	293.35	470.18	381.45	248.83	353.71	44.52	116.47
2	289.46	463.94	376.39	245.53	349.02	43.93	114.92
3	285.62	457.78	371.39	242.27	344.38	43.35	113.40
4	281.82	451.70	366.46	239.05	339.81	42.77	111.89
5	278.08	445.71	361.59	235.88	335.30	42.20	110.41
Total present value in perpetuity: $PV = 1/r$							
Total PV	22098.08	35418.51	28734.39	18744.43	26644.92	3353.65	8773.59

Note: $d = g-r$. $g = 5\%$, $r = 6\%$ (See Szenberg et al. 1977, 75).

Table 4.8 **Estimates of foreign elasticities, 1984–1998**

Independent variables	Single equation estimates		SURE equation estimates	
	Log(Impind)	Log(Expind)	Log(Impind)	Log(Expind)
Constant	–15.23	–8.58	–15.17	–8.62
	(–14.09)***	(–17.01)***	(15.75)***	(–19.36)***
Log(Relative Prices)	–0.88	–1.37	–0.94	–1.37
	(–1.86)*	(–2.12)**	(–2.27)**	(–2.46)**
Log(GDPDM)	2.24		2.24	
	(18.11)***		(20.26)***	
Log(GDPDC)		2.85		2.86
		(25.42)***		(28.89)***
R^2	.97	.82	.97	.99
D-W	.82	1.71	0.85	1.71

Note: Impind = Index of Imports; Expind = Index of Exports, GDPDC = GDP of Industrialized Countries. GDP= US GDP. Data are from the *International Financial Statistics* Yearbook, 1999.

---

[4] In James Meade's *A Geometry of International Trade*, the Production Possibility Curve (PPC) is sliding up a stationary indifference curve tracing out the countries' Trade Indifference Curve and subsequently, with the terms of trade defined, the Marshallian Offer Curves. In that process, the points of tangency of the PPC moves to a higher level of efficient gains from trade, but the point of tangency moves as well, indicating substitution effects between capital, labor, and goods between the home and host countries. Such gains can only be captured in a GE setting.

A Reconciliation of Computational General Equilibrium (CGE) Estimates of Benefits from the Economy's Liberalization

In the CGE models, tariffs enter indirectly via the effect they would have on consumption levels, and the estimate would be either static or dynamic, depending on whether or not we allow time for saving and investment to adjust to an equilibrium value. The specification we make for the GE computation aggregates trade between the United States, Canada, Mexico, and the Rest of the World (ROW). While more detailed models would bring out interesting share-vying characteristics, such as the Big Three losing shares of exports to China and Mexico during liberalization, our simple model focuses on the impact on the domestic economy within the NAFTA setting, where we concentrate our interest on TAA effects.

Relative to larger aggregations, such as those with 10, 12, or 24 sectors, our aggregation minimizes the complexities of substitution, and even distortions. Specifically, we expect that "if substitution possibilities are moderate, then the welfare costs of distortions will be small" (Dornbusch 1993, 86). According to Leontief (1953), interactions among the sectors that are aggregated in the net are reduced.[5] Consequently, we should expect a relatively smaller estimate of the welfare index. On the other hand, a welfare estimate from a larger aggregation would be incomparable and inconsistent, using the same logic with a PE estimate, and, therefore, would not allow for reconciliation. Further, if one allows for correlation of a small aggregation with small welfare gains, this would give credence to the argument that the large disparity between PE and GE estimates of welfare effects may be due to an increase in substitution and distortion complexities.

In estimating the welfare gains from liberalization in a CGE setting, we make the standard assumption that labor and capital are mobile, while land and natural resources are sluggish. Factor substitution would follow a constant elasticity of substitution (CES) specification. As with the PE model, we need to come up with GE estimates of elasticity. More often than not, GE models rely on the literature for elasticity, but in a few cases they use a methodology similar to that in the PE literature. They tend to use the popular Armington elasticity which specifies that partial elasticity of buyers' demand at home be dependent on the share of the foreign manufacturers in the home country's total expenditure on

---

[5]   Assuming we are consolidating firms 2 and 3, then "If firms 1 and 2 buy commodities or services from each other, as well as from other concerns, the new consolidated account will show purchases or sales from 2+3 to 2+3. This kind of registered internal turnover gives rise to the distinction between gross and net accounts. The former registers all the value transfers between the original simple accounting units, irrespective of any further grouping. The latter suppresses all transactions among the members of the consolidated accounting group. In other words, it reveals only the external relations and treats the newly formed groups as if they were the original firms and households" (Leontief 1953, 14–15).

manufacturers, on one hand, and the elasticity of substitution, on the other hand (Armington, 1969).[6] However, some CGE models, such as that of Abdelkhalek and Dufour, sought econometric estimates of elasticity, which are somewhat in line with the PE estimates we made above. Table 4.8 indicates our fit of that model for CGE elasticities. The import elasticities show no variation from –0.88, which we estimated in the PE approach using Szenberg's et al. (1977) single OLS methodology. However, it has increased to –0.94 in the SURE system of equation environment.

Another consideration for our CGE benefit estimate is the tariff rates. The GTAP tariff rates are computed from the input-output data for 1996. The benchmark data, which uses 9 per cent for textile, and 13.4 per cent for wearing apparels, are in line with the disaggregated rates of the USITC above. It was estimated by dividing the value of import tariffs (MTAX) by the sum of the values of commodity trade (VXMD), export tax (XTAX), and transportation services (VTWR). This estimate has a shortcoming. The GTAP database shows no data for MTAX for the textile and apparel sector from both Mexico and Canada to the United States. The USITC data indicate that while the estimate is positive, it was not zero. However, its small values, which Table 4.5 shows to be 0.84 per cent and 0.97 per cent for Mexico and Canada to the US, respectively, were incorporated into the CGE model. This reconciliation should not significantly change the overall benefit estimate as another USITC (1999) calculation would render the above 9 and 13.4 per cent estimates about 10 per cent above the 1996 average. The inconvenience of using average tariff rates is well documented in the literature.[7] They are, however, the most readily available estimates whose predictions are found acceptable in the area of commercial policy.

Using those elasticities and tariff rates, the CGE model must now proceed to the specifications of the utility and production functions. Here we followed Harrison et al., (1997) in assuming constant returns to scale (CRTS) for perfectly competitive markets, as increasing returns (IRTS) are not usually used for textile and apparel markets. More specifically, we assume constant elasticity of substitution (CES) of capital and labor, constant elasticity of transformation

---

[6]   Armington actually proposed two formulas:

1) $\eta_j^i = (1-S_j^i)\sigma^i + S_j^i \eta^i$ and

2) $\eta_h^i = S_j^i (\sigma^i - \eta^i)$ j ≠ h, where η_j^i = partial elasticity of demand of buyers in the ith country for output by the jth country, S = share of the jth country output in the ith country total expenditure, σ^i = elasticity of substitution in the ith market between the output of any two countries, η^i = partial elasticity of demand of buyers in the ith country, and η_h^i = cross elasticity with any other country. When the subscripts are not equal to each other we get import elasticity.

[7]   For example, Irwin noted that the average tariff rate is a "downward-biased" indicator since imports with high tariffs are not proportionately weighed; that it is further biased with the changing composition of imports when tariff rates are adjusted, and it changes even when the tariff rates do not change (*American Economic Review* 1998, 1016).

(CET) between domestic and exported goods and services, and CES for the final demand of the single, representative consumer. We summarize the requisite inputs for the CGE benefits computations as follows, dictated by the data available from GTAP Version 4, GEMPACK, and GTAP in GAMS software:

Regions	Industries	Factor assumptions	Substitution assumptions
US	Textile	Land—Sluggish	Households—CES
Canada	Wearing apparel	Skilled labor—mobile	Firms: base model—CRTS
Mexico	All others	Unskilled labor—mobile	Imports—CES—Armington
ROW		Natural resources—Sluggish	Capital—Mobile

We calibrated the model to the 1996 data, the latest period for which data are available. The calibration uses quantities to fix the indifference curves for each country, prices to fix budget constraints in line with those indifference curves, and elasticity of substitutions that identify particular indifference curves. In such benchmarking, it is standard procedure to check for standard equilibrium conditions across the countries. The cross check was done for several markets, including the following major ones (terms in brackets refer to GTAP variables):

1) Transport services: Subtracting the value of international transportation sales (VST) from the value of transport services (VTWR);
2) Imports: Commodity trade (VXMD) + transport service (VTWR) + import tariff = import less government inputs (VGM) plus aggregate intermediate inputs (VAFM) less value of domestic sales (VDM);
3) Investment and savings: investment (INVEST) less depreciation (VDEP) less savings (SAVE);
4) The Walrasian: Expenditures (EXPEND) less income (INCOME); and
5) Balance of Payments: Exports – net capital inflow – imports (VXMD+XTAX+ VST) – (INVEST-VDEP-SAVE) – (MD + XTAX + VTWR).

The table shows our simulated results of welfare benefits for various assumptions under steady state conditions, i.e., holding the capital stock to the base year level. The results indicate that the benefits range from a negative to a positive value depending on tariff rates and elasticity assumptions. The 2 and 4 per cent elasticities are in line with Harrison et al., multifiber arrangement (MFA) scenario. The lower estimates of 1.3 and 0.88 per cent are our estimates for the NAFTA-dominated period. Apparently, there is little convergence on the levels of these estimates. Rather divergent levels are appropriated for different scenarios. For example, Trela-Whalley used 30 and 15 elasticities, respectively, while Harrison et al. used elasticities as low as zero and 0.5 for CET. In this direction, Spinanger (1998, 9–10) has questioned the thoroughness of the computational CGE methodology for failing to take account of critical aspects of MFA and for the possibility of being misspecified.

The high variance in elasticity estimates has significantly different results. Harrison et al., found that the estimate of the elasticity of demand for textile and apparel products, when high, is critical to their estimate of benefits. In fact Harrison et al. (1997, 1405) stated: "We evaluate the elimination of the MFA and find that it results in losses for the developing countries as a whole, except when we assume implausible high elasticities of demand." The significance of this is that it does not deprive our PE estimate of any credence quality. Actually, a CGE range of benefits running from negative to positive values underscores our PE values as a valid estimate.

Based on the growth in the NAFTA countries, we surmise that it was not an efficient rate where all countries—United States, Canada, Mexico, and ROW, have reached a state from which they would not want to shift from their techniques of production. Rather, the post-1996 period indicates that the United States continued to specialize as demonstrated by further gains from trade. It is also possible to make that inference from the relative improvement of factor prices, not necessarily their equality, since we are dealing with diverse countries. However, that would require further GE analysis. We have sufficient indications here to lower the GTAP tariff rates by a tax multiplier of about 10 per cent to contain it within the limits of the above sources.

Table 4.9   Tariff rates sensitivity analysis

Variation in tariff rates of GTAP	CES between imported and domestic goods	CET between exported and domestic goods	Welfare benefits ($ billions)
Full	4	2	–$0.06
5% cut	4	2	$1.11
10% cut	4	2	$2.29
Full	1.37	0.88	–$0.01
5% cut	1.37	0.88	$1.25

Note: Full = GTAP rates with USITC Data for Mexico and Canada. Cut = reducing the GTAP rates. In particular the equation in the simulation was TM(.) = T(M) *(1-0.1) for a 90 per cent tariff multiplier (or 10 per cent cut).

Conclusion

TAA benefits to displaced workers make up a significant percentage of the costs that displaced workers bear in the import impacted garment industry. While early struggles with the concept were hampered by the "character of the postwar

American trade policy regime," it has now evolved into an indispensable link to sector-specific adjustment programs, and in the case of NAFTA, a tool to look out for the broader "national economic interest of the United States" (Hufbauer 1986, 33–41).

This investigation highlights the premise that TAA benefits are necessary and sufficient to extract the significant sizeable benefits from trade liberalization within the different political climates of the sample period. It invigorates the consumer surplus methodology in its PE manifestation. In order to compare this estimate with the more fashionable CGE approach in the literature, we have attempted reconciliation by restricting the CGE domain of aggregation. Such an effort makes the possible range of CGE estimates to include the PE estimate, lending credence to the latter that the current literature relegated. The overall results lend support to the anecdotal view that while the TAA benefits had a "slow go" in their inception, those benefits displayed a great stable upward trend during the NAFTA years.

"But for" TAA, the benefits of liberalization during the NAFTA period may not have been significant, based on the high per cent of relief to total costs. We have found that TAA benefits explain a significant per cent of the total cost to the garment industry, ranging from a low of about 14 per cent in 1981 to 67 per cent in recent years. The data show that the NAFTA years have witnessed a step-up of the TAA certifications over prior years, which approximates about 10 per cent higher than the cost-benefit levels in the peak years of the 1980s (Table 4.3, Col. 20).

Note

The import and export time series are taken from various annual reports of the USITC, "US Imports of Textiles and Apparel Under the Multifiber Arrangement" and from USITC data web. The quantity data for the SIC 23 group was most consistently available by kilograms for exports and square yards for imports. The Office of Trade Adjustment Assistance provided TAA data. GTAP data for the 10×10 model were taken from Yang et al., GTAP data for the 12×12 and 24×24 was provided by Harrison et al., GTAP NAFTA was aggregated from the GTAP version 4 database using GTAP in GAMS software from the University of Colorado

Chapter 5

The Steel Industry

Industry Background and History of Foreign Competition

The United States Steel industry underwent a major paradigmatic shift between the 1950s and 1990s. In the 1950s, it was characterized by its emphasis on production; in the 1990s, it was characterized by quality and costs (Hall 1997, xiii). Downscale of size from "Big Steel" to "Minimill," "Born Again Mills," "Flat Rolled Minimills," and "Integrated Mills" of the 1990s was widespread. High concentration and vertical integration characterized the early phase, while diversification characterized the latter. In 1952, four firms (US Steel, Bethlehem, Republic, and Jones & Laughlin) accounted for 61.3 per cent of US Basic Ingot Capacity (Bain 1959, 129).

According to Stigler, the integrated steel industry (Ingot) had a fairly high level of concentration at the time US Steel was formed. The Herfindahl index (the firm's share of the sum of squares of shares of industry output) was at 0.233 when a number of companies merged to form United States Steel in 1901. That share steadily declined to 0.122 in 1960 (Stigler 1968, 264, 284). The share of the dominant firm also declined, from 60 per cent in 1910, 40 per cent in 1935, and 23 per cent in 1969 (Shepherd 1997, 88, 105). A major reason for the decline is that the industry had negligible product differentiation, which was limited to customer service and personal sales representation, which also meant negligible entry barriers (Bain 1956, 124–7).

Some argue that the great transformation in the industry was not a function of easy entry alone. According to Tornell (1997), the transformation can also be attributed to protectionism, high wages, low investment, new entrants, and failure to adopt new technologies. He argues that the industry did not implement new technologies that were available; the high prices from protection, about 15 per cent increase, were not matched by productivity increases. In fact, productivity declined by 45 per cent while the ratio of steel to United States assets fell from 56 to 19 per cent between 1976 and 1990. Further, the shares of small firms increased from 15 to 39 per cent during 1970–1989 while demand fell by 22 per cent. Let's consider these issues in the price and non-price context with some historical background.

Pricing Strategies

According to Marengo (1955, 509), the steel industry used "a multiple basing point system" for pricing its products until 1948. (The issue was whether to base prices at a single point (Pittsburgh) or at multiple points (Pittsburgh, Cleveland and Chicago). "Pittsburgh was the point of surplus production of Steel, whereas Chicago and other points did not produce enough to satisfy their local demands; therefore, the Pittsburgh price plus freight was the *natural price* determined by supply and demand." However, "steel actually made at Chicago was sold as though it were made in Pittsburgh, and ... the freight that was added was not the *actual freight* from Chicago but the imaginary freight from Pittsburgh" (Hekman 1978, 127, 510). Issues regarding natural price and actual freight cost overshadowed import impact issues in the early days of the industry. Competition was focused at the "point of delivery," and not at the "point of manufacture" (Commons 1924, 511). However, either due to domestic firms' complacency or due to the dynamics of foreign competition, "Steel imports increased from a trickle of mostly low-quality products in the 1950s to a large supply of high-grade steel in the mid-1950" (Adams 1995, 100), and the industry appeared to have been caught off guard.

As the industry evolved, the domestic firms added auxiliary considerations to its price strategy, to administer prices with stepwise increases as a rule, and only fallback to the basing-point strategy as the exception (Adams and Dirlam 1964, 627). However, the firms remained keen on competition, matching one another's prices in a lock step manner. Perhaps this was a mistake, for through thinking that competition is price rather than non-price, the industry "forgot" foreign competition; foreign firms recognized that "any fool" can match a price cut, and started to innovate in the non-price gambit areas.

From the 1970s to the current period, imports have disrupted the uniformity of the price system to the extent that it provoked retaliation against countries. During that period, the share of US imports averaged approximately 20 per cent compared with approximately 5 per cent in 1960 (Adams 1995, 100). Various administrations responded with restrictive trade agreement to cushion the effects of imports. First, we note the effect on prices of the Voluntary Restraint Agreement (VRA) during the 1969–1974 period.[1] Between 1960–1968, the steel price index rose 4.1 points; between 1968–1972, 26.7 points (ibid., 104). Second,

---

[1]   Steel Voluntary Restraint Arrangement (VRAs) is a formal agreement between the United States and the governments of 16 countries plus the EC. Although the structure of the arrangements varied, exports to the United States of both carbon and specialty steel products were restricted either to a specified quota or to a percentage of US import penetration, based on quarterly estimates of U.S. domestic consumption. The VRA program was initiated for five years beginning October 1, 1984, and was subsequently extended in September 1989 for 2½ more years. The last VRA program terminated March 31, 1992 (Source: http://usinfo.state.gov/products/pubs/trade/glosssz.htm#steelvolres).

we note the effect of the Trigger Price Mechanism (TPM) of 1978–1982.[2] This method allowed minimum price fixing on imports, but opened the door for innovation in the non-price areas to foreign firms.

Non-Price Strategies

Adams and Dirlam identify two non-price avenues for the steel industry to react to import competition (1964, 646). One was that United States firms were lagging behind the world in using technology such as the basic oxygen furnaces (BOF) and continuous casting technology. The other was that the firms could seek protection through lobbying. We will look at each in turn, both from the state of the economies and world competitive points of view. The literature charges that the leading United States firms failed in technology rivalry with foreign firms. An equally valid view, we argue, is not the failure to retaliate, but the role of both the firms' cash flow and the United States economy in precipitating the crises of the 1980s. As explained in an interview with the United Steel Workers' president Lynn Williams (Kaufman 2001, 145–71), the demand for steel in the early 1980s was increasing. The industry was capital intensive, enjoying lucrative profits, and industry officials felt that there was no need to change the technology. However, incidents such as the OPEC shock and the appreciation of the dollar have made imports cheaper, making it appear that it was a mistake by the firms not to modernize in the first place. In order to follow this line of reasoning, we have advanced hypotheses under the headings of technology and politics.

Trade Adjustment Assistance for Steel

The US ITC made several recommendations for tariff imposition on imported steel, alongside TAA (US ITC Report: EC-Y-046, Investigation # TA=201-73, November 21, 2001, Table Flat 4). These recommendations seemed imminent in the face of dumping from abroad that accounted for nearly half of the antidumping cases, 201 of 451, filed between 1980–1989. In 2004, President Bush lifted the temporary tariff protection he had placed on imported steel.

---

2   TPM is a system for monitoring imported steel to identify imports that are possibly being dumped in the United States or subsidized by the governments of exporting countries. The minimum price under this system is based on the estimated landed cost at the US port of entry of steel produced by the world's most efficient producers. Imported steel entering the United States below that price may trigger formal antidumping investigations by the US Department of Commerce and the US International Trade Commission. The TPM was in effect between early 1978 and March 1980. It was reinstated in October 1980 and suspended in January 1982. Between April 1982 and June 1988, TPM was used for imports of stainless steel round wire only.

We investigate the effect of TAA in the steel industry because the amount of relief a petitioner receives is related to the cost of trade-tariff imposition, voluntary export restraint (VER), quotas, or trigger price mechanism. Staiger and Wollock (1994b, 101) document that the relief that petitioners obtain from import impact can amount to "about half of what they might expect from a positive final determination and duty imposition." Similarly, Melo and Tarr (1990, 493) found that the removal of Quantitative Restrictions (QR) on the steel industry during 1985 amounted to about 0.86 billion of 1994 dollars (1990, 493). At that time it was also found, based on various elasticity assumptions, that about 20,700 jobs were lost to the industry, and about 23,300 persons were relocated industry-wide, due to the removal of QR.

To find that there is net welfare benefit in the face of import impacted unemployment may at first appear to be inconsistent with trade liberalization activities. This inconsistency is expected because the literature on the industry includes inconsistent and somewhat contradictory statements that invite reconciliation. For example, we find statements such as, "steel is an oligopoly in the horizontal sense," followed by "The steel industry is, of course, vertically integrated as well" on the same page of major analytic studies (Adams and Dirlam 1964, 638). Or, for example, the statement, "The existence of substantial and variable backlogs contradicts the view that the industry maintains excess capacity" (De Vany and Frey 1982, 441). We have witnessed controversies about the nature of price discrimination in steel between Stigler (1942) and Blair (1943). More recently, an econometric model addressed issues as to whether it was cost or demand factors that enabled the industry to grow with centers in Pennsylvania, Ohio, and Illinois-Indiana (Hekman 1978, 123).

The number of persons and petitions certified and denied for the steel industry is presented in Table 5.1. In terms of certified petitions and workers, the steel industry accounts for 509 and 68,181, respectively. The number of certified steel workers is surpassed only by the auto 600,653 and garment industries 355,471 in our set of distressed industries.

Table 5.1 indicates that between 1994–1999, the years of the Clinton administration's early experience with NAFTA, 106 petitions covering 16,421 employees were certified. After NAFTA about 1 per cent fewer petitions and employees (4.17 and 4.81) were reported annually than before (6.09 and 5.84). Similar downward trends were observed for the US ISFTA and US CAFTA, indicating an even larger decline in per cent certified than with NAFTA. Superimposed on this is the fact, presented in Table 5.2, that the rates of duties declined during the NAFTA years, from 4.09 per cent in 1994 to 3.0 per cent in 1997, and 2.2 in 2001. However, note that Table 5.1 also shows that the annual per cent denials also decreased, 1.33 for the NAFTA period versus 7.18 for the prior years for petitions, and correspondingly 1.14 versus 12.82 per cent for employees.

Table 5.1 Petitions and employment experience of various free trade hypotheses, 1980–1999, the steel industry

Years	Petitions				Employees			
	Total certified	Total denied	Annual % certified	Annual % denied	Total certified	Total denied	Annual % certified	Annual % denied
1980–1999	509	1,141			68,181	214,340		
Data for NAFTA comparison:								
1980–1993	403	1,065	6.09	7.18	51,760	207,279	5.84	12.82
1994–1999	106	76	4.17	1.33	16,421	7,061	4.82	1.14
US ISFTA comparison:								
1980–1986	271	765	8.87	11.17	35,138	162,771	8.59	21.82
1987–1999	238	376	3.90	2.75	33,043	51,569	4.04	3.46
US CAFTA comparison:								
1980–1984	181	668	8.89	14.64	24,531	142,353	8.99	28.62
1987–1999	238	473	4.60	2.96	43,650	71,987	4.57	4.14

Table 5.2 Primary metal products, calculated duties for all countries for united states imports for consumption

Year	Calculated duties	Dutiable values	Duty rates (%)
1989	594,648,294	15,287,107,382	3.889867973
1990	566,128,528	14,036,030,841	4.033394728
1991	516,040,762	12,561,832,642	4.108005390
1992	505,778,810	12,557,892,923	4.027577023
1993	524,696,240	12,705,330,333	4.129733161
1994	706,115,436	17,283,496,085	4.085489605
1995	640,025,352	17,630,231,864	3.630271893
1996	621,238,520	18,783,599,357	3.307345457
1997	594,631,231	20,099,589,694	2.958424724
1998	572,291,732	19,227,927,270	2.976356858
1999	413,020,745	15,906,004,348	2.596634176
2000	428,784,304	18,076,490,012	2.372055104
2001	306,788,593	14,000,800,506	2.191221801

Source: Compiled from tariff and trade data, US Department of Commerce, US Treasury, and the US International Trade Commission.

In the remainder of this chapter, we postulate hypotheses to be tested for both partial and general equilibrium points of view.

Technology

We start out with the hypothesis that the United States firms failed to modernize.

Hypothesis 1 (Adams and Dirlam 1964): *The modern steel industry has been lethargic in adopting new technology.*

The problem started in the 1970s. On the demand side, the first OPEC crisis of 1973 initiated a switch to more energy efficient cars that used a lesser per cent of steel. Engine blocks and head, doors, hoods, and bumpers were increasingly made with aluminum, fiber and plastic substitutes. The OPEC crisis was repeated in 1979, and was followed by a deep recession in the early 1980s. Along with the OPEC crisis came several recessions that slowed demand in the construction industry, a large buyer of steel. The crises were dominant from the early 1970s to the early 1980s. In 1982, more than 200,000 steel workers were laid off. We also note that the switch to lighter body cars continued into the 1990s. For instance, in 1994 the International Iron and Steel Institute (IISI) called for Ultra Light Steel Auto Body (ULSAB).

On the supply side, recycling gained headway. Its effect in transforming the industry was probably equiproportional for steel and aluminum products (*Steel Times*, April, 1997, 135). But it did offer smaller firms such as Nucor the opportunity to enter the industry.

Political Non-price Strategy

Hypothesis 2: *Firms in countries with smaller world share would be more aggressive in the R&D front, and would license their technology freely in order to break up or make inroads into the leader's market share.*

Corollary to Hypothesis 2 (Adams and Dirlam (1964, 67) Lenway et al. (1996), Morck et al. (2001): *Steel firms that expect losses from trade would not only make forward looking adjustments to their investment in R&D, but would tend to lobby for protection in a habit forming way.*

Adams and Dirlam (1967, 917) placed technological innovation in the domain of a "response to" and "not a cause of" import competition. Therefore, the leading firms in the United States were expected to retaliate to foreign competition. What in fact we find is:

1) A lag in the response, which was about two years for small firms, and much longer for large firms; and
2) That small United States firms such as McLouth Steel in the 1950s and Nucor in the 1980s were leaders in the lagged response to foreign technology.

This "response to" theory is true for foreign firms in reaction to the US firms. For example, the LD converter was invented in Austria in 1950, adopted in Europe in 1952, in Canada in 1952, and in the United States in 1954 by a small firm with one per cent of the market share, McLouth Steel. United States Steel adopted it in 1963; Bethlehem in 1964, and Republic in 1965 (ibid., 1967, 917–18). Again, the modern inventor of thin-slab casting, which took place in 1984, was SMS, a West German firm. Although SMS was willing to license its technology, only one small United States firm, Nucor, adopted it two years later, 1984 (Ghemawat 1997, 146–7).

Large firms' response to losing share to imports was not complacency. We must recognize the Schumpeterian axiom that large firms are always involved in continuous technological progress. This axiom, however, bears the theory that larger firm's incentive to lead in adopting interim technology is expected to be weak (Ghemawat 1997, 152). When the thin-roll technology was made available by SMS, the United States giants were in a strong profit position, and given their capital intensiveness, were maximizing returns on their existing technology (Kaufman 2001). This is also the early contention of Slesinger who argued that the conventional method was competing well with newer technology, and therefore, should not be scrapped (Adams and Dirlam 1966, 165). When that theory failed, the US firms turned to the government for political relief. Some of the recent political gains noted above include: quotas imitated by the Reagan and Bush administrations under the umbrella of the Voluntary Restraint Agreement (VRA), and the Trigger Price System. But this benefit of protection to large and small firms did not benefit large and small firms symmetrically. According to Lenway et al. (1996), firms have different propensities to lobby, and their aim may be directed in large part to appease their stockholders. Morck et al. (2001) have argued that such lobbying is habit forming.

Besides the strength of firms, and their propensity to form lobbying habits, we would like to identify and study those lobbying activities that are driven by purely economic forces. First, the statistics show that import competition has created many inroads into the market share of the American iron and steel industry, creating a steady stream of displaced workers, and governmental policy responses through TAA. Over the last 50 years, the share of imports to apparent consumption has increased from 1.5 per cent in 1950, to 4.7 per cent in 1960, 13.8 per cent in 1970, and 16.3 per cent in 1980 (American Iron & Steel Institute Data). By 1985 it had reached more than 30 per cent, which prompted the ITC to recommend protection from foreign imports to the Reagan Administration. The administration sought voluntary restraint solutions.

Second, dumping activities also provoked a response from the steel industry. According to Boltuck and Litan, 201 of the 451 antidumping cases filed between 1980–1989 were accounted for by the iron and steel industry (1991, 3). However, this appears to have been a peak period, for the *US News & World Report* (Oct. 12, 1998, 55) argued that share of cases for the steel industry dropped to about a third over the previous 20 years to about 236. As a result, the steel industry had been characterized by three phases of protectionist actions: voluntary export restraints (VER) (1969–1974) trigger price mechanism (TPM) (1978–1982), and a combination of VER and TPM (1982–1984), (Chung 1998, 151; Morck et al. 2001, 365–7).

Some argue that the steel industry would be complacent without strong import competition. With import competition, the steel industry is forced to modernize, keep excess capacity under control, and reduce increases in wages. Protection would not allow these to happen, and would result in secondary effects on other industries. For example, in the metalworking industries, this would lead to a larger multiplier effect (about 10 times that of the steel industry) on GNP, due to its larger workforce. But in this milieu of action-reaction in the open steel industry, it is hard to identify what the benefits and costs are to the whole economy. For this reason, some analysts had turned to general equilibrium analysis for an estimate. But they have not been able to weigh in the effect of TAA benefits into their analysis. In this study, we take the first steps in this direction, through assessing the welfare benefits to the consumers after TAA benefits awarded based on import impact are considered.

Trade Liberalization

The industry is currently confronting competition occasioned by free trade under GATT/WTO. As of 1996, the U.S. and world economies were protectionist. Traditional CGE models lump the steel industry with other industries (Melo and Tarr, 1990). But Chung (1998) has argued that the steel, chemical, and food industries were most affected by Section 701 (countervailing duty), and Section 703 (antidumping duty) of the trade remedy laws, which should justify a study of them in isolation. Examining GTAP data base shows that the value of antidumping duties was $63.3 billion for steel and iron, $852.4 billion for machinery, $2,450.6 billion for chemical rubber and plastic, and $587.5 billion for the food industry. These industries accounted for 90.8 per cent of the total antidumping duties, which was $4,356.3 billion that year. That share in the former Soviet Union was 75.5 per cent, in Europe 86 per cent, and in Latin America 84.4 per cent. The corresponding percentage for ordinary import duties was 77.7 for those industries in the United States, while export subsidies were approximately 16 per cent. The high percentages of duties accounted for by those few industries warrant studying them independently, as suggested by Chung.

Models and Estimates of Welfare Benefits due to Liberalization

The traditional model of welfare benefits seeks a net benefit estimate through consumer surplus via trade liberalization. One approach takes the PE estimate which does not consider interaction with other industries besides steel. Its methodology follows from an estimate of the triangular consumer surplus area under the demand curve within the framework of a price tariff adjustment, $P(1+t)$, captured by the formula: $\frac{1}{2}(t^2)0_mV_m$, where t is the tariff rates, 0_m is the price elasticity of imports, and V_m is volume of imports. The GE estimate, on the other hand, postulates interaction with the world either through a single or a block of countries, interacting over different levels of aggregation over commodity groups. The traditional Pareto optimality condition occurs when no one in society strictly prefers a broad bundle of commodities, say B, to a unified bundle, say A, and at least one person in society prefers bundle A to B. A quasi-ordering of choices (reflexive and transitive), including variation of assumptions on dominance conditions postulated by Kaldor, Hicks and Scitovsky, or by Chipman, Moore, and Samuelson, can under a compensation schema return to equilibrium after a disruptive state in the economy. We can consider what kinds of transfer payments such as TAA benefits to different states of the economy, Ω, is appropriate to sustain the economy. In the case of steel, we witness how governments alternate between trade liberalization efforts under NAFTA to various restrictions such as VER, quotas, or trigger price mechanism, including the recent March 2002, Section 201 move by President Bush to have a temporary (18 month) 30 per cent hike in tariffs, prompted by a recommendation of ITC and other lobbying efforts by the steel industry. Our research investigates the effect of the compensation payment benefit level to displaced workers, say TAA, in the different states of the economy, TAA ε Ω, to work with the set of potential states, TAA*$\subseteq$ Ω, that would keep the economy going if not in an optimal state.

Partial Equilibrium Benefits Estimates

Both PE and CGE estimates require elasticity data. The PE estimates utilized the tariffs and import values indicated in Table 5.3. The import elasticity is the average indicated in Table 5.7, viz., –0.60. The US ITC positive benefit was arrived by using the upper end of the elasticity.

Table 5.4 presents the PE estimates of costs due to displaced workers. Gross labor costs without TAA benefits is estimated at $117.38 million in 1994 and $85.99 million in 1997. After subtracting benefits from the TAA program, the net labor losses were reduced to $73.67 million in 1994 and $68.01 million in 1997.

With the standard assumptions that the economy's potential growth rate is $g = 4$ per cent and that its discount factor is equivalent to the five-year Treasury Bill rate of approximately $r = 6.333$ during 1994–1997, we can get a discounted value of $d = g - r$. Using the tariff rates, t, discussed above, and the corresponding

Table 5.3   Parameters and estimates of US ITC vs PE estimates

Products	Duties: ranges	Elasticity of domestic demand supply	Elas. of sub. between United States and imports	Net benefit estimates at 30% tariffs (in $000)	Sources: US ITC
Carbon and alloy:					
1 Flat	1.1 to 2.8	DD:–0.3 to –0.8 SS: 3 to 6	3 to 6	–$90,862 to–$2,154	EC-Y-046: pp. Flat: 2,3,4,10,21
2 Long	1.0 to 3.2	DD:–0.5 to –0.75 SS: 3 to 5	2 to 8	–$16,855 to –$4,081	Ibid., Long-4,20, 29
3 Tabular	0 to 6.2	DD: –0.5 to –1.0 SS: 3 to 5	4 to 6	–$41,270 to $4,127	Ibid., Tabular-1,15
Stainless steel	0 to 6.2	DD: –0.25 to –0.75 SS: 4 to 7	2 to 5	–$354 to $4,919	Ibid., Stainless-2,3,4,5,30,44.
Average	0.60				

volume of imports, Vm, we can get a partial estimate of consumer surplus. Table 5.5 indicates that trade liberalization has generated a consumer surplus of $366.96 million in 1994 and $223.78 million in 1997. Taking out the labor displaced costs for the two years is substantial, $4,925.74 million and $3,608.5 million, indicating the small relief TAA has given to the trade impacted burden during the NAFTA globalization period.

General Equilibrium Benefits Estimates

We will consider various levels of aggregation of commodities and countries in a general equilibrium estimate of benefits under different states of the economy, mainly liberalization and tariff states. We created a 2 × 4 aggregation, which separates the iron and steel industries from all others. The four groups of countries include the US, Canada, Mexico, and the rest of the world (ROW). Within this first model, we also aggregate the NAFTA group for comparison with other aggregations. This aggregation emphasizes the recent Section 201 ruling to the effect that the NAFTA countries are not affected by the 30 per cent tariff hike. The estimates were done for the years 1995 and 1997 based on the availability of GTAP data. Coincidentally, the US ITC recommendation contains many references to that period as the desired period to set the recommended tariffs and quota level for benefits and competitive considerations (US ITC, EC-Y-046, Table Flat 4). Model 1 indicates the benefits assuming no retaliation from the rest of the world, and no trade liberalization as of 1995.

Table 5.4 Estimates of losses due to NAFTA and TAA

Cost estimates:	1994	1997		Reference
Displaced workers:	4905	3234	T	Office of TAA
Denied	2296	2268	Z	
Certified	2609	966		
Hourly wage	16.13	17.63	A	AISI Table 5, 1999 (Regular hours)
Average weekly hours worked	41.70	42.40	B	Ibid., Table 6
Yearly earnings:	34,974.12	38,859.60	C	USITC, 1999, 30 (other manf.)
Weeks remained unhired	22.80	22.80	D	Ibid.,
Per cent permanent unemployed	0.07	0.07	E	Ibid.,
Years left before retirement	3.90	3.90	F	(Szenberg et al. 1977)
Total loss for certified and denied:				
Number permanently displaced	348.26	229.61	G=T*E	
Income lost for 3.9 years ($M)	47.50	34.80	H=(F*G*C)/$1M	
No. unemployed for 22.8/52 (years)	1997.96	1,317.31	I=(1-E)*(D/52)	
Income lost for 22.8/52 (years)	69.88	51.19	J=(I*C)/$1M	
Total loss without TAA	117.38	85.99	H+J	
Assistance provided by TAA:				
No. certified displaced permanently	185.24	68.59	K=Z*E	
Income received for 3.9 years ($M)	17.69	7.28	3.9Kx.7C	
No. remain unemployed for 22.8/52 (years)	1,062.73	393.48	L=(1-E)*(D/52)	
Income lost for 22.8/52 (years)	26.02	10.70	M=L*.7C/$M	
Total benefits of TAA	43.70	17.98		
Net labor costs	73.67	68.01		

Table 5.5   Costs and benefits in the steel industry

Time	PV benefits		PV costs with TAA		PV costs without TAA		Losses with TAA		Losses without TAA	
	1994	1997	1994	1997	1994	1997	1994	1997	1994	1997

Present value from $PV = \frac{1}{2}(t^2)Elas_m \, V_m (1+d)^i$:

Time	1994	1997	1994	1997	1994	1997	1994	1997	1994	1997
Value	8.74	5.33	73.67	68.01	117.38	85.99	(64.93)	(62.68)	(108.63)	(80.66)
1	8.54	5.21	71.96	66.43	114.65	83.99	(63.42)	(61.22)	(106.11)	(78.78)
2	8.34	5.09	70.28	64.88	111.98	82.03	(61.94)	(59.79)	(103.64)	(76.95)
3	8.15	4.97	68.65	63.37	109.37	80.12	(60.50)	(58.40)	(101.22)	(75.15)
4	7.96	4.85	67.05	61.90	106.83	78.26	(59.09)	(57.04)	(98.87)	(73.41)
5	7.77	4.74	65.49	60.45	104.34	76.44	(57.72)	(55.71)	(96.57)	(71.70)

Total present value in perpetuity: $PV = 1/r$:

	1994	1997	1994	1997	1994	1997	1994	1997	1994	1997
	366.96	223.78	3091.71	2,853.97	4,925.735	3,608.474	(2,724.75)	(2,630.20)	(4,558.77)	(3,384.70)

The first part of Table 5.6, Model 1 indicates that as of 1995, the state of US trade with the rest of the world yielded $21.149 billion in welfare benefits, which would increase to $21.189 billion with a 30 per cent tariff hike on steel imports from the ROW (excluding Mexico and Canada) without trade liberalization. With the larger aggregation of Section II, which has 11 commodities (i_s=steel, crp=chemical, food, machinery, metal, mvh=motor vehicles, textile, wearing apparels, cns=construction, others, cgd=capital goods) and 9 listed regions, the benefits are somewhat smaller, $20.102 billion and $21.480 billion, respectively. The smaller benefits are due to distortions. As we introduce more distortions into trade, the benefits drop, but the gains from protection increases by $0.4 billion (21.189–21.149) in Model 1, and $1.378 billion (21.480–20.102) in Model 2. The central finding is that the United States stands to gain about $0.4–1.4 billion from a 30 per cent tariff hike, ceteris paribus.

Data for GTAP5 indicate that trade relationships do not stand still. A re-estimation of Model 1 with 1997 data indicates that the benefits fell dramatically, from $21.149 billion in Table 5.6–Model 1 without tariff hike to $12.350 billion indicated in Table 5.7. However, the 1997 data indicate that a tariff hike of 30 per cent on steel imports would cause benefits to increase from $12.350 to $12.390 billion, adding only $0.04 billion (12.39 – 12.35). Without re-running Model 2 with the new data, we can infer that the benefits seem to be falling over time even without retaliation from the ROW, perhaps explaining why the current Bush administration made it only a temporary hike with a three year lifespan.

Table 5.7 also considers scenarios under which the world can retaliate against the United States' tariff hike. It indicates that the increase in tariffs for all United States products to the ROW, excluding Mexico and Canada, need not be proportional. If the ROW were to retaliate with a 25% increase in tariffs, then the United States would be thrown back to its pre-tariffs benefits levels of $12,350 billion.

Comparison of our CGE Benefits Estimates with the US ITC Remedy Report Estimates

The GTAP estimates for 1995 and 1997 indicated a downward trend in benefits. The decline of benefits from $21.189 billion to $12.390 billion in 1997 with a 30 per cent tariffs hike, projected to 2000, would be $7.244 billion in 1998, $4.236 billion in 1999, $2,477 billion in 2000, and $1,448 billion in 2001. The US ITC released several reports on its findings of import impact on the steel industry. It reported benefits and remedies under four broad product groups (US ITC: *Steel*, Publication 3479, Volume 1, Determinations and Views of the Commissioners, December 2001, 23):

1) carbon and alloy product flat products;
2) carbon and alloy long products;

Table 5.6   CGE welfare benefit models, 1995

Regions	1 (2×4): Individual rationality: steel vs. other industries; United States, Canada and Mexico vs. ROW.				2 (11×9): Detail model:			
	Benefits Tmult.=1	Benefits ΔTmul.	% change	Regions	Benefits Tmult.=1	Benefits ΔTmul.	% change	
USA	$21.149B	21.189	0.19	USA	20.102	21.480	6.42	
Canada	$0.606B	0.617	1.78	Canada	0.557	0.734	24.11	
Mexico	$0.782B	0.784	0.26	Mexico	0.754	0.842	10.45	
NAFTA	$22.536B	22.590	0.24	NAFTA	21.413	23.056	7.13	
ROW	$30.763B	30.688	-0.24	Europe	18.058	17.397	-3.80	
World	$53.299	53.278	-0.04	ASP	11.308	9.894	-14.29	
				FSU	1.279	1.253	-2.08	
				AFR	0.593	0.626	5.27	
				LAC	0.097	0.105	7.62	
				ROW	0.494	0.555	10.99	
				World	53.260	52.886	-0.71	

Note: Assumptions: CES of capital and labor; CET between domestic and exported goods, and CES for the final demand of the single, representative consumer. Sluggish land and natural resources, mobile capital, and skilled and unskilled labor. The tax multiplier is set to 1 in the first column, and 1.3 for steel imports from ROW (excluding Mexico and Canada) for the second column.

Table 5.7   CGE welfare benefit model, 1997

Regions	Benefits Tmult.=1	Benefits ΔTmul.	% change
USA	$12.350B	12.390	.32
Canada	$1.577B	1.590	.82
Mexico	$1.889B	1.893	.21
NAFTA	$15.816B	15.872	.35
ROW	$42.453B	42.359	–.22
World	$58.269B	$58.231	–.07
Benefits to the United States as a function of % world's retaliation:			
10% World's retaliation		$12.374	
20% world's retaliation		$12.358	
25% world's retaliation		$12.351	
30% world's retaliation		$12.343	
40% world's retaliation		$12.328	

Note: Model 1. (2x4): individual rationality: steel versus other industries; United States, Canada, Mexico versus ROW.

3) carbon and alloy pipe and tube products; and
4) stainless steel and alloy tool steel products.

Its benefit estimates relate prices, quantities, revenues, consumer costs and welfare to tariffs, quotas or tariff rate quotas (TRQ) equivalent for the year 2000, under a no-growth scenario (US ITC, EC-Y-046, November 21, 2001, 3). Table 5.6 indicates positive benefits only when the upper range in the elasticity assumptions are used. Average benefits in that case would be $2,743 million (average of –2,154, 4,081, 4,127, and 4,919). In other words, our estimate of benefits in 2000 of $2.5 billion approximates the US ITC estimate of $2.7 billion.

Conclusion

The United States steel industry has struggled against globalization and technological changes during the last two decades. This is evident enough from the government efforts to protect the industry from foreign competition in line with recommendations emanating from the new trade theory. Liberalization has significantly lowered import duties, cutting it by nearly half from its 1994 level of 4.8 per cent rate. The consequence of increased foreign competition has led to increased consumer welfare benefits that are not recognized by PE estimates.

The PE estimates of welfare benefits for the steel industry indicate that TAA benefits were not able to cover the impact from liberalization of trade during the NAFTA globalization period. However, a CGE investigation indicates that the PE benefit estimates may be biased downwards because substitution with other industries is not allowed in a PE environment. Overall, welfare benefits for the country have been positive as predicted by free trade theories, but the industry had to undergo huge restructuring. For instance in "April 2002, W.L. Ross & Co. purchased the steel mills of LTV Corporation in Cleveland, then added Acme Steel Corporation, the Bethlehem Steel Corporation and Weirton Steel" (*New York Times*, October 26, 2004). Yet this does not seem to be the solution for the United States Steel industry as there is talk about additional global mergers and continuing drama that will motivate further study in the future.

Chapter 6

The Pharmaceutical Industry

Introduction

Most studies embed pharmaceutical firms within firms in different industries in studies of innovation, prices, and returns to make up for sample size and to infer aggregate industry performance from market structure. But the industry structure appears fragmented at best, with waves of mergers occurring to confront globalization and intellectual property rights (*The Economist* June 23, 2001). Information about the structural direction that the industry will take resides within the brain cells of the CEOs of major companies.

In Chapter 1, we found that the endogenous growth model predicts nonrivalrous behavior for R&D behavior in a national and global setting. This information translates into process and product innovation at the level of the firm, where R&D, advertising, and productivity are the driving forces for success. We have collected time series from 1980–1999 for seven firms: Abbot Laboratories, American Home Products, Bristol-Myers Squibb, Eli Lilly, Merck, Johnson and Johnson, and Pfizer to investigate rivalry among them. We statistically fitted four equations corresponding to four hypotheses and found that smaller firms tended to set their R&D and advertising budgets taking Merck's previous outlays as given. However, when Total Factor Productivity is investigated for the same period, large firms tend to react to small firms, reaffirming concerns in the literature regarding size versus innovation.

Background

The US Pharmaceutical Industry has enjoyed economies from the aging baby boomer population, aggressive R&D, advertising and productivity efforts, and now from the opportunities available in the global economy. The potential opportunities and challenges for pharmaceutical innovations are tremendous. Groundbreaking advances in technology have led to unprecedented pharmaceutical discoveries. Yet a major concern is that regulations by the FDA will generate low returns to investments in R&D. For instance, the rate of return in the late 1970s fell by a third to its 1960 levels, and the cost of discovering and developing new drugs increased 18-fold (*Business Week* February 21, 1977).

During the 1980s, the pharmaceutical industry received a boost from the Reagan administration that lengthened the patents on prescription drugs and hastened the pace of approving generic drugs to substitute for drugs with expired patents. The immediate result in the 1980s was that R&D expenditures in drugs was about 10 per cent of the industry's sales, versus 3 per cent for all manufacturing industries (S&P *Industry Survey* January 1985, H16). But the FDA's Center for Drug Evaluation and Research (CDER) still regulates the industry brand name, generic prescription and OTC drugs, placing a heavy time delay on production. The time it takes to develop a new drug has almost doubled from its 1960 levels. The actual trend is 8.1 years in the 1960s, 11.6 years in the 1970s, 14.2 years in the 1980, and a stable 14.9 years during 1990–1996 (*Pharmaceutical Industry Profile* 2000, VI). CDER claimed that with the user-fee approach in the mid-1990s, where the applicant pays the government for its review, they have doubled the number of new drugs approved and halved the review time (*FDA Consumer* September–October 1997, 21). Other policies such as the streamlining of the IND and the International Conference on Harmonization also reduced review time. However, the review time continues to generate concern. The industry's strategy is:

1) To have an ample supply of R&D projects and patents in the pipeline;
2) To lobby Congress and get extension of time on their patents in order to recoup their investment costs;
3) To allow the speedy approval of generic drugs in order to substitute for drugs whose patent has expired; and
4) To make drugs available before approval in special cases such as the HIV epidemic in South Africa.

Globalization Effects

At the firm level, big changes such as NAFTA have not noticeably affected firms in the pharmaceutical industry relative to firms in other industries such as the textile, shoes, autos, and steel industries. An early concern on the international scene was the debate between Canada and the US over compulsory licensing of firms' pharmaceutical patents (Hufbauer et al. 1992, 173, 179). This issue seems to be resolved within the framework of The Agreement on Trade-Related Aspects of Intellectual Property Rights (TRIPS) under WTO that grants 20 years patent protection for pharmaceutical and other products. Today, the international scene is populated with demonstrations, such as in Seattle in December 1999 against the WTO and others against the G8. These demonstrations are not so much related to free trade as to issues of fairness, transparency, and environment (*JAMA* June 12, 2001, V285, i22, 2844). Other specific concerns hover around generic pricing as it relates to South Africa. In that situation 39 drug companies tried to stop the importation of cheaper medicines and the substitution of generics, as was permitted under TRIPS. However, the lawsuit was dropped due to global political pressures on the companies.

On the employment impact side, competition from abroad has made little dent on the market of domestic firms. This might be because American firms dominate the global market, where six of the top 10 firms are based in the United States (S&P *Industry Survey* June 28, 2001, 9).The statistics show that over the 1980–1999 period, pharmaceutical companies have filed only 28 petitions with the International Trade Commission (ITC), covering 4,535 employees, of which most were denied (20 with 3,906 workers) and few were approved (eight with 629 workers). Perhaps the reason for the small import impact had been that pharmaceutical companies have always been on guard against foreign competition. They use strategies such as drug licensing, joint ventures and mergers to counter foreign competition. The push for intellectual property rights through the WTO's TRIPS rules illustrates the former.

Beginning in the mid-1980s, the pharmaceutical industry has been characterized by larger and more frequent merger and acquisition activity. The threat of patent expirations has influenced the increased merger activity within the industry. Many pharmaceuticals with high sales histories fear losing their patent protection and face competition from generic copies. There has been evidence that sales can decrease by as much as 75 per cent in the year preceding patent expiration. Through merging with other industry players, pharmaceutical companies are able to pool their advertising, R&D, and productivity efforts while simultaneously cutting costs.

While the literature has extensively assessed prices, profits, and R&D efforts, advertising and productivity efforts were generally given a lower profile. These issues were considered by the Kefauver Committee in 1962 and again by the Subcommittee on Monopoly in 1976, which noted that "The drug industry has vast resources at its disposal. Its expenditure for advertising and promotion of drugs is now well over $1 billion per year or about $5,000 per physician per year" (Subcommittee 1976, 1395). Considering that advertising outlay is substantially greater than R&D outlay, and that long-term productivity is a major source for its economic growth, it is surprising that the study of advertising and productivity have taken a back-seat in the literature.

In this chapter we develop four hypotheses and associated corollaries in order to perform an integrated analysis of seven major firms in the pharmaceutical industry. The model section develops these hypotheses around the concepts of scale economies, R&D, advertising, and Total Factor Productivity. The rest of the paper is divided into sections on the statistical results of at least four equations that were developed to evaluate the hypotheses with data.

Model

Traditional models focus on how prices and quantity in a market are determined. The pharmaceutical industry is useful for investigating price and non-price competition. Commenting on Caves et al. 1991 article, Pakes (1991) wrote that it is "cleaner" than most related industrial organization problems for several reasons. First, there is a legal monopoly for the first T years of the product's existence, and then free entry occurs at a fixed sunk cost thereafter (the cost of approval by the Federal Drug Administration), giving us a well-defined set of rules to determine possible market interactions. Second, it is reasonable to argue that there are common and fairly constant costs of production for the drugs being sold. Third, after the introduction of the branded drug, there seems to be only one major type of investment (advertising), and we have reasonably detailed data on it. There is, however, a difficult set of economic problems in modeling demand and in defining precisely what we mean by "brand loyalty" (Pakes 1991). We model the pharmaceutical industry from its price and non-price aspects, and bring out rivalry among the major firms within this framework. No one model is broad enough to account for all of these activities, hence we begin with some simple abstraction, namely that the firms arrive at a pricing strategy through non-market means, and that the firms rely heavily on non-price competition for their survival.

Fudenberg et al. (1993) provide the essence for a model in the form of a time game where a firm's strategy set includes a time to either "stop" or "not stop" their efforts, which can include pricing, R&D, advertising, and productivity efforts. A firm can, for instance, lower its R&D cost to C, from a higher level, C'. Assuming its rivals do not react, the firm will expect a stream of benefits V(t) from such research efforts. Such a formulation allows one to estimate social gains if a social gain function can be specified. Scherer (1967) was one of the earliest to advance such a model within a profit maximization framework to predict a firm's market structure. He gave it an exponential form, which was further expanded by other authors. Reinganum (1984) has summarized some of those models to derive stylized facts about a firm's size, excess capacity, strategies for increasing or decreasing efforts in equilibrium, leadership role, pre-emption strategies, and licensing. Some of the modern features of the exponential model are summarized in Tirole's book (1997, ch. 10). Rather than developing the model here in symbolic form for each of the variables, we next discuss the form it takes in the estimation of each of the price and non-price categories.

Price Competition

On the demand side, the consumer is not the one that usually makes the choice of using a particular drug. Mostly, drugs are prescribed by physicians, who sometimes lack the necessary information about relative prices (Ellison et al. 1997, 437). Consumers, in attempts to gather or aggregate decentralized information, may want to free-ride on information from another patient that has already gone through that experience, the so called "herd" behavior effect (Choi 1997, 409–10).

On the supply side, pricing strategies are complicated by the fact that a firm can transfer or license encoded experience to other firms (Levitt and March 1990, 24). The tendency has been for firms in developed countries to press their government for strengthened patents regulation in foreign, particularly less developed, countries. Domestic manufacturers claim that they can sell abroad at higher prices if patent laws are strengthened. Even developed countries that trade with the US were reluctant to agree. Canada signed a law in 1987, allowing 7–10 years exclusivity to new drugs from abroad. Several other developed nations, including Japan and the EC, have pledged to adopt more uniform patent laws recommended by the Uruguay round of negotiations under GATT. The Agreement on Trade-Related Aspects of Intellectual Property Rights (TRIPS), under the WTO seeks minimum 20 years patent protection for pharmaceutical products, which should be in full effect by 2006.

Models on the global scene have demonstrated that price discrimination is evident in the industry's performance. Schut and VanBergeijk (1986) have argued that where patents are allowed, higher prices are expected to prevail. On the other hand, lower prices are expected if competition is encouraged, if the market is large, and if price control is practiced. Levy (1999, 74) offers several "competing explanations for observed price differences. Differential pricing may be the result of increased opportunities for price discrimination or may reflect the presence of quality or cost variations in different segments of prescription drug markets." It seems that price discrimination and differentiation are driven by cost, product amenities, and not just by the vulnerability of a certain segment of the population which can afford it.

Price competition is further complicated by the presence of generics. After considering the pros and cons for increase or decrease in brand versus generic pricing, Scherer concluded that the most likely scenario is "for the incumbent to maintain or increase its price, while ceding a substantial share of the market to much lower-priced generic rivals" (1993, 101). Such complications are also present in the pricing of "me too" drugs, which are variation of drugs already in the market place, "orphan" drugs that do not have a parent company, and "OTC" drugs.

It is clear that the pricing of pharmaceutical products is not the result of spontaneous or induced market forces. Forces internal to the cost structure of the firms and external to the firms' organizational structure contribute to price formation. The idea of price discrimination is high on the hierarchy of pricing strategies related to brand versus generics, and across international trading partners that adopt varying degrees of foreign patent protection.

Non-Price Competition

Concerns about non-price competition focuses mostly on R&D and patents, and somewhat less on advertising, sales promotion, and productivity. On the

R&D side, the central thesis of the "exogenous growth" point of view under non-price competition for the pharmaceutical industry is Schumpeter's argument that innovation is a public good that must be encouraged by a patent system. However, from the endogenous growth point of view, the R&D sector is primary. To produce a new chemical entity (NCE) or a new molecular entity (NME), the pharmaceutical manufacturer must lay out a substantial portion of R&D expenditures, estimated over $500 million, seek patents for its invention, and advertising to promote knowledge of its product.

The pharmaceutical industry holds the special dishonor in that the cost of patent protection for this industry is about three times the commercialization of innovation relative to petroleum, machinery, and fabricated metal products, and far more relative to autos or textiles (Mansfield 1986). Firms, however, are not dissuaded by the cost barrier. We enumerate some of the reasons of this in the literature, with a view to be able to specify a statistical model for non-price competition in the pharmaceutical industry, as follows:

1) Patents are arranged long enough to allow returns to cover R&D outlay. This has been the foundation of the Waxman-Hatch Act of 1984;
2) Competition seems to be driven by the "Patent First" initiative. This has been modeled in a gaming situation between two firms—one leading, the other following. Fudenberg and Tirole (1993, 123) argue that "it is optimal for each player in such games to stay in until discovery once his opponent has quit;"
3) It is not easy to imitate a good discovery. Successful imitation requires substantial learning (Mansfield 1968). Specialized imitation models were examined for the drug and auto industries. Grabowski (1968) has investigated imitation in the pharmaceutical industry along with the chemical and petroleum industries; and
4) Models of R&D follow a memoryless, Poisson state, implying that if there is any reaction at all, it is immediate (Tirole 1997, 384). It implies that lagged R&D may not be a good specification for a rivalry situation such as that advocated by Grabowski and Baxter (1973). We will examine this lagged aspect empirically around the central thesis of this paper, which is with regards to the imitation feature of firms, whether they react to a leader or just to each other.

Although "endogenous growth" models classify R&D as a nonrivalrous good, we find tremendous rivalry among firms. However, we do find that this industry is a good example of willingness to cooperate with the government by paying higher patent review fees in order to speed up the patent approval process. In close concert with this collaborative effort detailing and sales promotion efforts are also important for the industry after R&D. According to Caves et al. (1991), "The pharmaceutical innovators have two principal instruments, price and sales-promotion outlays, for maximizing the value of their innovations, both during the period of exclusive marketing and in the post-entry game" (Caves et al. 1991, 5).

We observe that the large companies spend up to three times on marketing as they do on R&D. Detailing requires the firms to maintain a large staff, and hence high fixed cost, in order to inform the medical profession about the firm's product. It accounts for about three quarters of the firm's promotion outlays.

In an integrated model, we also examine rivalry from the Total Factor Productivity (TFP) perspective of the firm. This aspect is posed in the form of whether "basic research, as contrasted with applied research and development (does) make a significant contribution to an industry's or firm's rate of technological innovation and productivity" (Mansfield 1980, 863). As presented, this model requires a distinction between basic and applied R&D, which is not generally available to firms. Mansfield estimates that the per cent of R&D expenditures for basic research declined from 20.7 to 15.3 per cent between 1967–1980 in the drug industry, and points out that the latter forecast are not data consistent with the earlier ones (ibid., Table 2). A more detailed view will distinguish between "product" versus "process" knowledge, implying that "firms are even willing to reduce the quality of their products to increase productivity," in cases where they would standardize their product (Thompson and Waldo 2000, 158–159). Following Mansfield (1988, 223), we will use R&D expenditures as a measure of the firm's R&D capital, without the basic and applied distinction. We then concentrate on "process" knowledge measured by TFP in the sense of Thompson and Waldo.

In sum, we have formulated the following hypotheses to enable our statistical investigation.

Hypothesis 1 (Scherer and Ross 1990, 657–658): *Economies of scale and timing games are important for pharmaceutical firms' choices, behavior, or survival.*

While economies of scale in production are not important for the pharmaceutical industry, based on the small scales nature of fermentation processes (Caves et al. 1991, 8), they are important from the R&D and promotion side. The literature, to our knowledge, has neglected this line of research. Following Scherer (1999), we provide the analysis for firms' R&D outlays. It requires fitting the firm's R&D expenditures on the firm's sales, either through a linear or polynomial specification. The mere fact that R&D expenditures may escalate as rivals compete to get a patent first on a new product makes such a study necessary. We note that, subject to diminishing returns, the expected completion date of a project can be shortened through a firm's increasing R&D expenditures, which also underscore economies of scale. Also, because patents can be licensed to rival firms, R&D outlays can spillover since the research findings of a firm is available to others free of charge, a sort of external economy. Scherer also underscored the view "that advertising, by making known the availability of new products, enables innovators to tap larger markets more rapidly, enhancing the profits from innovation and hence strengthening incentives for investment in innovation" (Scherer 1980, 378).

The Grabowski and Vernon (1977, 361), and Scherer's (2001, 657) industry studies advocate regression analysis to establish reaction patterns between innovational output, such as R&D or patent and sales, in linear and polynomial form. Grabowski and Vernon have tried innovative output linearly on sales alone, including a polynomial up to the third degree. They were only after a good fit, reporting an R^2 of 65 per cent. Scherer advocated only a second degree polynomial, which is consistent with Grabowski and Vernon's specification. We have decided to adopt the latter, which implicitly involves fitting the following equation:

$$\text{Output} = f(\text{Sales}, \text{Sales}^2) \qquad\qquad \text{Eq. 1}$$

Hypothesis 2 (Griliches 1990, 1702): *Patents are good indicators of differences in inventive activity across firms.*

Corollary 1 to Hypothesis 2: *Patents are an output and R&D an input to the firms' rivalry process.*

Corollary 2 to Hypothesis 2 (Tirole 1997, 394): *Efforts to obtain a patent via R&D expenditures proceeds in a "memoryless" or "Poisson" state.*

The hypothesis requires a test for association between a firm's R&D expenditures and the number of patents. This relationship sheds light on the innovation process and technical change. Cross-sectional statistics explain differences in a firm's inventive activities. However, rather than correlating just R&D with patents, we will expand on this model in the direction of rivalry, i.e., pitting one firm's R&D outlay against another, taking into consideration the number of patents the firms received in the previous period. In symbolic form:

$$\text{R\&D}_{it} = f(\text{R\&D}_{j(t-1)}, \text{Patent}_{i(t-1)}), \qquad\qquad \text{Eq. 2}$$

where i is the ith firm, j is the rival firm, and t is time. The above specification resembles Grabowski and Baxter's (1973) model, except that we substitute patents as an independent variable for their previous period R&D expenditures, and have dropped some collinear variables.

In Corollary 1, we intend to use a firm's patent award in the previous period in order to cut through the controversy of whether a patent is an input or output. According to Kamien and Schwartz (1975, 4), R&D is an input and patents are an output in the innovation process. We may think of an R&D input as generating an R&D output as diagrammed by Hay and Morris (1979, 444). Many authors have used it as a measure of a firm's capital for innovative input. Mansfield separates it into basic research and applied research capital and uses it as inputs in a firm's production function to explain total factor productivity (Mansfield 1980, 861). Grabowski and Baxter (1973) have advocated the use of a firm's R&D

expenditures in the past period. However, because its influence may be dominated by previous patent awards, we use patents instead. Our substitution of patents as an independent variable in place of R&D in this context has other purposes as well. We use the patent variable in a conditional probability sense. A firm might, in the most naïve sense, want to forecast its current level of R&D outlay based on current information. However, if some information is gathered on the firm's past patent's award and effectiveness, the firm may want to incorporate that information into its decision making on R&D as well, thus making a conditional probability forecast.

In Corollary 2, our use of patents is also instrumental in throwing light on the "memoryless" or "Poisson" game of the firm's race for a patent. According to Tirole (1997, 394), in such a model, "a firm's probability of making a discovery and obtaining a patent at a point in time depends only on this firm's current R&D expenditures and not on its past R&D experience." As stated above, the literature for the specification of equation 2 above would require that we put a lagged $R\&D_{it}$ variable in the place of patents. A significant statistic on such a variable would act as a potential falsifier of this "Poisson" model. In fact, we find that the patent variable does perform better.

On the empirical side of the literature on R&D rivalry, Grabowski and Baxter (1973) have demonstrated for eight firms in the US chemical industry that rivals do react to the R&D outlays of other firms, when other determinants such as cyclical movements are controlled. They argued that firms do not match R&D expenditures as precisely as they do advertising. In an earlier work for the chemical, petroleum and drug industries, Grabowski (1968) discovered that such reactions proceed with a one period lag. However, the pharmaceutical firms made up only a subset of that sample. This study, on the other hand, exclusively considers pharmaceutical firms.

Hypothesis 3 (Grabowski and Mueller 1969, 1970, 1971): *Advertising competition among pharmaceutical firms leads to imitation of their advertising expenditures.*

The pharmaceutical industry advertising budget has received attention since the Kefauver-Harris Act of 1962 noted that the industry is spending more on advertising than on R&D. Today, the pharmaceutical firms have about six major channels to target advertising expenditures: detailing, sampling, direct mailing, journal advertising, general media advertising, and ads directed at physicians for continuing medical education (Schweitzer 1997, 48). According to Measday (1977), "No other products on the market are promoted as intensively as ethical drugs," and ethical drugs had been the faster growing segment of the industry relative to proprietary drugs.

The traditional—perhaps antitrust—view of advertising is that innovative firms engage in large amount of advertising and promotional expenditures, which act as a barrier to entry for new and small firms. Another view is that advertising sells invention such as new discovery, or the molecular imitation of a rival's new product. Although the way the literature treats advertising hypotheses are not well-formed for statistical investigation, we find that this aspect of the industry has received a fair share of research (Comanor 1986, 1196). For instance, in his interpretation of the advertising effect of generic drugs on brand, Frank et al. (1992, 173–4) notes that "The econometric model of advertising and market share yielded estimates of the impact of number of sellers on the advertising effort of the leading firm." Another study by Caves et al., was primarily concerned with the relationship between advertising and the rate of return to R&D. We see the basis in these early studies for an imitative work in advertising among the rival firms. Accordingly we have formulated the following specifications for the investigation of Hypothesis 3.

$$\text{Advertising}_{it} = f(\text{Advertising}_{j(t-1)}, \text{Cashflow}_{i(t-1)}), \qquad \text{Eq. 3}$$

where i is the ith firm, j is the rival firm, and t is time.

Hypothesis 4 (Comanor 1986): *Firm size may have an influence on technical advance.*

This hypothesis involves the use of R&D activities as a measure of a firm's new products, and sales of new products as a measure of a firm's marketing activity. One issue here is how to separate the effect of advertising and sales promotion (Comanor 1986, 1191). We first estimate total factor productivity for the seven firms in our model using the following specification for each firm over time:

$$Q = Ae^{\lambda t}R^{\alpha}L^{v}K^{1-v} \qquad \text{Eq. 4}$$

where Q is the firm's value added, A is a measure of TFP and its growth rate, R is R&D capital, L is labor, and K is capital. We then proceed to measure total factor productivity (TFP) via the equation $\text{Log}(Q/L) - v\text{Log}(K/L) - (1-v)R/L$ for each firm. We integrate advertising into the sales and R&D hypothesis by using to calculate TFP instead of R&D in Eq. 3, and jointly estimate them with the advertising specification in Eq. 4.

Equations 2, 3, and 4 above take the Cobb-Douglas-type production function form, relating R&D and advertising, and indirectly TFP, to the firm's previous rival's outlay, conditioned on the firms current states of patent awards and cashflow, respectively. They are dynamic in that they involve lags and purport to show the influences of the firm's changing states of patents and cashflow over time. Ordinarily, in a production like specification, the constant term would capture the firm's process technology, and advertising would make known to the public the product quality of the firms. However, such interpretation would be placed in the background until now where we introduce the traditional input of capital and labor in our estimation of the TFP model. The main issue we pose to estimate with these specifications is that each firm would generate in a simultaneous manner, R&D, advertising, and "process" knowledge in order to enhance the quality and growth of their product, with an eye on their rival's previous level of performance.

Results

In this section, we first investigate the relationship between economies of scale to R&D and patents for the seven firms. We then consider the rivalry question among firms. We also study R&D, advertising and productivity in an integrated manner.

Scale Economies

Table 6.1 presents our results of Eq. 1 above. It underscores that the inclusion of the constant term is necessary because they turned out mostly significant. In the fit of Grabowski and Vernon, the t-values were insignificant for both the linear and non-linear forms. This is the case for our results for only American Home Product where the coefficients of –157.79 in the patent, and 169.07 in the R&D equation, were insignificant. In the case of Pfizer, only the constant for patents, viz., 57.82 was insignificant. The other constant terms are significant.

The linear sales coefficients are significant for 8 of 14, implying that 6 of 14 are negative. Of the nonlinear coefficients, only 8 are significant, and half are positive indicating increasing returns. Adding up significant intercept and nonlinear coefficient, 5 of 14 are significant indicating constant returns. Four nonlinear coefficients are positive indicating increasing returns, which means that five of which some are insignificant are indicating decreasing returns.

Compared with the Grabowski and Vernon results, whose sales coefficient in the linear model was 0.74, and 0.94 in the polynomial equation, our results are small, ranging between –0.006 for Pfizer, to 0.27 for Lilly. The sales coefficient was -0.88×10^{-3} in Grabowski and Vernon, which is in the vicinity of what we find. Their R^2 of 0.64 compares with ours, which are mostly in the 80–90 per cent range.

Non-Price Rivalry Results

The results in this section explain competitive reaction among the seven firms for market share or dominance. The contribution here is that pharmaceutical firms do compete with each other from the R&D and advertising perspectives. We first examine the rivalry from the possibility of the leader and followers hypothesis. This requires us to identify one firm as the leader among the seven. The literature is unanimous on this. We therefore examine all the pairs of firms,

Table 6.1   Sales and innovation

Dependent	Constant	Sales	Sales^2	R^2	DW
Abbott: Pat.:	184	−0.07	0.000001		
¶	(10.95)***	(−9.06)***	(10.80)***	0.89	1.42
R&D:	−157.79	0.12	0.000002		
	(−7.03)***	(12.15)***	(0.17)	0.99	1.94
Am.: Pat:	−0.55	0.04	−0.000001		
¶	(−1.31)	(2.35)**	(2.01)**	0.11	1.07
R&D	169.07	−0.06	0.00001		
	(1.26)	(−1.36)	(3.69)***	0.97	0.70
Bristol: Pat.:	17.94	0.005	−0.0000001		
	(1.81)*	(1.64)*	(−0.54)	0.84	1.88
¶	−468.76	0.20	−0.000006		
R&D	(−2.91)***	(3.96)***	(−1.86)*	0.96	1.36
Johnson: Pat.:	46.71	−0.001	−0.0000001		
	((2.09)**	(−0.10)	(−0.31)	0.38	2.44
¶	−175.29	0.10	−0.0000004		
R&D	(−2.19)**	(5.33)***	(−0.41)	0.98	0.67
Lilly: Pat.:	203.43	−0.045	.000004		
	(4.71)***	(−2.27)**	(1.90)**	0.49	2.32
¶	−429.24	0.27	−0.00001		
R&D	(−3.12)***	(4.18)***	(−1.37)	0.98	2.57
Merck: Pat.:	211.35	−0.03	.000004		
	(6.61)***	(−2.38)***	(4.01)***	0.81	1.80
R&D:	−117.69	0.15	−0.000003		
	(−3.36)***	(11.90)***	(−2.72)***	0.99	0.97
Pfizer: Pat.:	57.82	0.006	−0.0000001		
	(1.36)	(0.35)	(−0.06)	0.34	2.13
R&D	150.49	−0.06	−0.00002		
¶	(2.18)***	(−2.01)**	(−8.08)***	0.99	0.94

Note: R&D and sales data are from Standard and Poors Industry Surveys, various years, and also available from the Compustat Tapes. Patent data are from the US Patent and Trade Mark. Full Text and Image data base (http://www.uspto.gov). The ¶ below the dependent variable indicates which of the two equations performed better from the statistical point of view.

namely 42 ((7!/(7–2)!) = 42 in our model. We perform the examination for the two main rivalry weapons, advertising and R&D, in a SUR model in order to take care of inter-correlation about the residuals as a consequence of the firms being in the same industry.

   We begin our estimation by looking at the literature for some guidance as to whether we can identify a leader, unambiguously. Scherer (1993), for instance, talks of Merck as a leader. Further, in his book, Scherer (1999, 65) expresses deep concern with the relationship of R&D and market outlays within the context of uncertainties about market acceptance. He mentions that firms are involved with both consumer and rivals' reactions to their product. "Although marketing research can provide some clarification, most of the uncertainties remain until well after the majority of R&D investment, and indeed, appreciable equipment and marketing roll-out investment, has been shouldered."

Traditional selection criteria would suggest that the examination of winners versus losers among R&D outlays, the size of the firm's portfolio of R&D projects, the number of patents awarded to stop imitators will give the innovating firm an advantage in recovering R&D expenditures. Indeed, some studies that look at the return to R&D suggest that the returns are highly skewed to a few top innovators. In their 99 new drugs study, for instance, Grabowski and Vernon (1990) found that the top 10 deciles of 99 new drugs received about 55 per cent of the profits, measured in terms of sales less cost of production, including marketing and distribution costs. This result also implies that the size of the portfolio of R&D projects is not a good measure of leadership because success will be skewed to only a few projects. We therefore fall back on the historical role of the firm, complemented with a few rule-of-thumb descriptive statistics to suggest a leader. Afterwards, a few cross-checks, such as bootstrapping and alternative discrete choice models, are performed to examine the robustness of the choice.

In Search of the Historically Dominant Firm

New medicines and vaccines derived from R&D efforts play an essential role in the progress of treatment of various forms of disease. Since the turn of the century, many causes of disease have been eliminated, and Americans of all ages have experienced progressive increases in life expectancy and improved overall health. Although drug trade and the use of plants and minerals for medicinal purposes date back several centuries, the industry began to have a noticeable presence beginning in the early 1930s.

Introduction of the first sulfa drug in 1935 led to an increased interest in pharmaceutical research and opened up the market for the launch of penicillin. 1938–1953 was coined "The Age of Antibiotics" as many new drugs were introduced to the market. In World War II, there was a great need for safe and easily administered drugs to protect wounds from infection. Although Alexander Fleming discovered penicillin in 1928, he was unable to produce the antibiotic in sufficient quantity to be of any clinical value. Twenty years later, Howard Florey and Ernst B. Chain produced solid penicillin and searched for vendors to produce the drug commercially. With the assistance of the United States government and several United States pharmaceutical firms, penicillin became the first commercially produced drug. After penicillin became a commercial product, it became evident that investment in the industry could lead to substantial profits and resources were allocated towards intensive research discovery.

Over the years, antibiotics and vaccines were important in the abolition of polio, measles, and other diseases. According to a PHRMA Study (Profile 99) of 152 major drugs developed between 1975 and 1994, 45 per cent were developed in the United States. Staggering death rates for various diseases in the 1920s have decreased over the years as the industry has developed.

Historically, the most important discovery has been penicillin, which was discovered in 1928 by Alexander Fleming. Because it was not patented, it was licensed freely by governments. Merck and Pfizer were early producers that enjoyed a sizeable mark-up over cost advantage. But the original price of $6000 per billion units in 1945 fell to about $100 and reached $15 by 1962 when entrants were able to penetrate the market (Meadsley, 267). Following penicillin, the next most important discovery was antibiotic, in particular tetracyclines that combat a wider range of organisms than penicillin. According to Scherer (1990), Pfizer held the markup advantage of about $60 per 100 tablets bottle. From this historical sketch, therefore, both Merck and Pfizer were leaders in the penicillin revolution, with Pfizer dominating in the post-penicillin antibiotic revolution. We now should take a look at the more current positions of these two firms to find out if other leading role reversals are present.

Some Descriptive Statistical Measures of Lead Role Reversals

Advances in biomedical science have helped pharmaceutical researchers develop new drugs and cures to attack various diseases. A PHRMA Industry Study (www.searchforcures.com/publications/industry) of R&D expenditures and sales have provided the following results:

1) R&D expenditures by research-based pharmaceutical companies have increased by 14.1 per cent between 1998 to 1999, reaching about $24.0 billion;
2) Over our sample period of 20 years, the percentage of United States sales allocated to R&D has increased from 11 per cent to 20.8 per cent. Meanwhile, the average R&D-to-sales ratio for all United States industries is less than 4 per cent;
3) Total drug development time has increased from an average of 8.1 years in the 1960s, 11.6 years in the 1970s, 14.2 years in the 1980s, to 14.9 years for drugs approved during 1990–1996;
4) About 350 fifty new biotechnology medicines (produced by 140 companies) are in the pipeline for development; and
5) Effective R&D requires an exorbitant amount of capital in order to succeed. A Boston Consulting Group estimate states that the pre-tax cost of developing a new drug in 1990 was $500 million, which includes the cost of research failures in addition to interest costs over the life of the investment. As the length of time needed to develop the drug increases, so do the costs. These costs of capital increase as pharmaceutical companies are exposed to economic risk

and uncertainty over a longer period. In addition, since the cost of developing new drugs is so expensive, commercial success is usually possible only for a few products, therefore, companies concentrate their R&D efforts on fewer products.

To help in the assessment of leadership, we have tabulated some descriptive statistics on the seven companies below. While Merck and Bristol-Myers are not far apart in R&D, Merck is clearly the leader in terms of sales force, median number of patents registered over the sample period, number of products, and market share. It is interesting to note that the company's percentage change in R&D is typically less than the percentage change in the industry's R&D during the sample period. It implies that smaller firms in the industry are making larger percentage expenditures on R&D in order to keep the industry's percentage change above those of the firms in our sample. The large firms' first preference is not to escalate their R&D expenditures above the industry percentage, perhaps with a view to avoid R&D wars. Their second preference is to keep the change in their R&D outlays in line with the industry's level of change, which demonstrates a Cournot type rivalry. Further, Merck chooses not to beat the industry's percentage as indicated by the fact that it has done so only one time in 19 years.

Pfizer, which shows aggressive historical dominance as discussed above, is low on the time series of R&D and patent trend, with a median of $585.5M and 90, respectively. It has the dominant effort in domestic sales force, 7,600, which may mean that it wants to use sales promotion strategies in order to bring up its market share, which is now below Merck's. Because some of the data in market share and list of products are missing, we can only conclude that it appears that Merck and Pfizer dominate. However, to leap to a conclusion that they lead the industry would be a hasty conclusion. We therefore will consider all the rivalry combination between any two firms in their competition in R&D and advertising expenditures in order to shine more light on the leadership hypothesis, which underscores that the firms engage in non-price over price competition.

Statistical Results on R&D

Although Merck leads in both the historical and size measure points of views, we plan to see how each firm responds to each other's lagged level of expenditure. Table 6.3 gives the rivalry results for the 42 different combinations of the firms in an R&D rivalry situation. The model that generates this result is from Hypothesis 2 above, effectively a combination of specifications from Grabowski and Baxter (1973) and Griliches (1990). A novelty of our approach is that firms make R&D outlays in a rivalrous domain in order to be the first to get a patent.

One notable feature of the results is that the rivalry does not proceed in a memoryless state via the Poisson probability distribution for success. In fact the firms do remember their lagged period's award of patents, which they put side-

Table 6.2   Descriptive statistics of a firm's dominant position in the industry

Company names	R&D median ($M)	US sales force 1999	Patent median (#)	Top 20 list of products 1995	Firms' vs. ind. R&D			Market share	
					Less than ind.	Equal to ind.	Greater than ind.	1996	1998
Abbott	534.5	2,759	88	7	10	5	4		
American	357.3	3,600	51		13	3	3		
Bristol	835.0	3,912	56	9	12	4	3	4.8%	5.3%
Johnson	776.5	5,000	38		11	4	4	4.0%	
Lilly	654.0	2,300	95	6	11	2	6		4.3%
Merck	802.5	5,000	219	17	12	6	1	7%	7.6%
Pfizer	585.5	7,600	90	6	6	7	6	4.6%	5.9%

Note: The median is over the sample period 1980–2000. Top 20 list from Schweitzer (1997, 24). Market Share is from *Chemical Market Reporter*, 10/04/99, 1. Sales Force from Med Ad News: (West Trenton, NJ: Engel Publishing Partners, Various years, September issue).

by-side their rival's previous period R&D outlay in order to make a decision on their current period outlay of R&D. Although the advertising results are discussed separately in the section below, the R&D and advertising rivalry decisions are estimated jointly. The model has worked well in that most of the R^2 are in the 90 per cent range.

The results of Table 6.3 can be reviewed in seven clusters depending on which firm is positioned as the leader. The first cluster indicates that firms respond positively to Merck's previous period outlay of R&D outlay. The responses vary from 0.96 for Johnson & Johnson to 1.38 for American Home Products, and they are all significant at the 99 per cent confidence level. The average reaction for the six firms on Merck's outlay is 1.23, which indicates an elastic response overall, indicating that the firms will always tend to do more R&D than Merck's previous period outlay. The influence of Merck's previous period patent awards indicates an overwhelming negative influence on other firm's R&D behavior. The reacting firms exhibit strong level of complacent behavior in that when their patent awards are up, they tend to ease up on their current R&D outlay, even though their rival's previous period R&D might be up. This behavior underscores that getting a patent is as important as the literature underscores.

The second cluster indicates firms' reactions on Pfizer's previous period outlay of R&D, which are all significant at the 99 per cent level as well. However, we note some differences of reaction to Pfizer from what we saw for Merck as the leader. Only American Home Products reacts fully with a coefficient of 1.09. The other firms indicate partial reaction ranging from 0.54 to 0.84. American Home Product is also the loner in this cluster in complacency relating to patents awarded. The other firms react positively.

The other five clusters indicate reactions to Abbott, American Homes Product, Bristol-Meyers, Johnson and Johnson, and Lilly, respectively. That firms react positively in these clusters is not in question. However, full reaction is limited to only American Homes Products and Pfizer versus Abbott; Bristol-Meyers versus American Home Products; no firms versus Bristol-Meyers; all but Lilly and Merck versus Johnson and Johnson, and all but Johnson and Merck versus Lilly. Whether the reacting firms are complacent based on their previous period patent awards is less significant in these five clusters. We have 18 of 30 significant patent coefficients, of which 11 are with negative signs, indicating a dominance of the complacency hypothesis.

Overall, we find that firms are reacting to each other's previous period R&D outlay, indicating strong non-price competition in that area. However, we are able to underscore that they react to the apparent leader, Merck. The dictum seems to be that often firms tend to imitate strongly the moves of the apparent leaders. We have overwhelming confirmation that firms are happy with relative high past period award of patents. It allows them to be complacent about non-price competition by allowing them to ease up on their current period outlay of R&D.

Table 6.3   SUR regressions of firms' R&D outlays on rival's

Dep./Ind.	Constant	Rival's R&D (–1)	Own patent (–1)	R^2	DW
Abbott/Merck	–1.74 (–7.73)***	1.26 (34.19)***	–0.07 (–3.44)***	0.98	0.60
American/Merck	–2.85 (–6.13)***	1.38 (20.47)***	–0.03 (–0.87)	0.95	0.40
Bristol/Merck	–1.74 (–4.15)***	1.37 (16.32)***	–0.21 (–2.17)**	0.94	0.46
Lilly/Merck	0.37 (0.79)	1.03 (15.33)***	–0.14 (–2.00)**	0.92	1.41
Johnson/Merck	–0.5 (–0.25)	0.96 (32.61)***	0.14 (4.28)***	0.98	2.83
Pfizer/Merck	–1.49 (–4.71)***	1.36 (34.87)***	–0.22 (–4.18)***	0.98	0.59
Abbott/Pfizer	0.69 (2.30)***	0.84 (18.22)***	0.05 (2.71)***	0.94	0.22
American/Pfizer	–0.67 (–3.05)***	1.09 (34.48)***	–0.04 (–2.04)**	0.97	0.79
Bristol/Pfizer	0.16 (0.34)	0.54 (7.38)***	0.73 (9.12)***	0.86	0.27
Lilly/Pfizer	1.45 (4.57)***	0.75 (17.65)***	0.08 (1.39)	0.95	2.23
Johnson/Pfizer	1.78 (9.63)***	0.72 (25.29)***	0.11 (4.50)***	0.97	2.00
Merck/Pfizer	2.01 (16.62)***	0.71 (40.90)***	0.03 (2.05)**	0.98	0.24
American/Abbott	–0.68 (–1.71)*	1.06 (17.74)***	0.09 (2.54)***	0.93	0.35
Bristol/Abbott	0.50 (1.77)*	0.92 (17.00)***	0.09 (1.03)	0.96	0.53
Lil (ly/Abbott	1.08 (4.97)***	0.76 (15.73)***	0.01 (0.14)	0.92	1.54
Johnsn/Abbott	1.89 (9.43)***	0.73 (23.97)***	0.11 (3.77)***	0.97	1.69
Merck/Abbott	2.26 (16.09)***	0.75 (37.13)**	–0.03 (–1.27)	0.98	0.74
Pfizer/Abbott	0.16 (0.52)	1.00 (23.72)**	0.04 (0.97)	0.97	0.39
Abbott/American	1.45 (4.28)***	0.82 (14.81)***	–0.03 (–1.43)	0.91	0.24
Bristol/American	2.81 (5.14)***	1.09 (11.77)***	–0.72 (–8.17)***	0.77	0.39
Lilly/American	2.19 (6.48)***	0.69 (15.68)***	0.05 (0.61)	0.94	1.79
Johnson/American	2.20 (7.67)**	0.62 (13.25)**	0.22 (9.50)***	0.91	0.98
Merck/American	2.86 (12.51)***	0.67 (19.66)***	–0.03 (–1.31)	0.94	0.35
Pfizer/American	2.23 (8.55)***	0.96 (26.32)**	–0.04 (–9.32)***	0.97	0.76
Abbott/Bristol	0.94 (3.65)***	0.94 (23.73)***	–0.16 (–8.02)***	0.95	0.50
American/Bristol	–0.50 (–0.90)	0.92 (11.01)***	0.20 (9.12)***	0.83	0.37
Lilly/Bristol	0.87 (2.47)***	0.64 (14.01)***	0.34 (8.61)***	0.92	1.76
Johnson/Bristol	2.26 (7.08)***	0.69 (14.55)***	0.03 (1.28)	0.91	0.80
Merck/Bristol	2.41 (11.90)***	0.72 (23.89)***	–0.05 (–2.58)***	0.96	0.36
Pfizer/Bristol	0.37 (0.92)	0.92 (16.21)***	0.06 (1.97)**	0.91	0.24
Abbott/Johnson	–1.56 (–3.79)***	1.23 (19.28)***	–0.08 (–3.17)***	0.94	1.18
American/Johnson	–2.62 (–5.41)***	1.34 (19.29)***	–0.05 (–1.70)*	0.95	1.35
Bristol/Johnson	–1.44 (–2.69)***	1.27 (13.27)***	–0.12 (–1.22)	0.90	0.67
Lilly/Johnson	0.26 (0.60)	0.98 (16.12)***	–0.05 (–0.65)	0.93	1.66
Merck/Johnson	0.43 (1.79)*	0.94(26.22)***	–0.01 (–0.19)	0.97	1.88
Pfizer/Johnson	–1.79 (–5.71)***	1.30 (30.02)***	–0.08 (–2.22)**	0.98	1.89
Abbott/Lilly	–0.475 (–1.03)	1.08 (15.79)***	–0.06 (–2.26)***	0.92	0.94
American/Lilly	–2.76 (–5.26)***	1.33 (16.93)***	0.08 (2.11)**	0.93	2.20
Bristol/Lilly	0.08 (0.13)	1.06 (10.34)***	–0.11 (–1.24)	0.83	0.57
Johnson/Lilly	0.86 (2.16)**	0.81 (13.04)***	0.18 (6.26)***	0.92	1.82
Merck/Lilly	1.24 (4.01)***	0.87 (18.39)***	–0.03 (–1.66)*	0.94	1.42
Pfizer/Lilly	–0.87 (–1.92)**	1.24 (18.74)***	–0.14 (–3.79)***	0.95	2.00

Note: All variables are in logarithmic form. Numbers in brackets are t-values. Three asterisks represent significance at the 99% level; two, significance at the 95% level, and one, significance at the 90% level.

Statistical Results on Advertising

Table 6.4 contains the results for advertising. Again the results are grouped in seven clusters, based on each firm being given the opportunity to lead. Of the 42 advertising coefficients, 28 are significant, of which only the reaction to Lilly are of the incorrect (negative) signs. The size of the significant advertising coefficients on Merck is 0.23 to 0.78; Pfizer is 0.32 to 0.39; Abbott is 0.27 to 106, Bristol-Meyers 0.66 to 2.10, Johnson and Johnson 0.69 to 1.45 and Lilly is –1.1 to 0.39.

Focusing on the signs for both the advertising and cashflow coefficients helps us to narrow down the leader in the case of advertising rivalry. This is suggested by the fact that while all of the advertising coefficients are significant with Johnson and Johnson as the leader, the results of the cashflow variable for that case are not supportive. They are significant only for American Home Products and Lilly, but the signs are negative rather than being positive. The joint cases where both of the coefficients are significant and are of the correct *a priori* signs is one for Lilly, two each for Pfizer, Abbott, and Bristol, and three each for Merck and American Home Products as leader.

There are criteria that would make advertising leadership swing between Merck and American Home products. Using size of the advertising coefficient in the joint cases, the American Home Products will come out ahead with the vector of advertising coefficient of [0.78, 0.74, 0.60] versus the vector [0.23, 0.37, 0.37] for Merck. However, using R^2 for the joint cases, Merck's average will be 0.93 (0.92+0.95+0.92)/3), and American Home Products' average will be 0.83 (0.83+0.91+0.93)/3), which is lower, thus giving the leadership to Merck. We also note that while American Home Products is reacting to Merck, Merck does not react to American Home Products. This asymmetry further tilts the leadership towards Merck.

Both the R&D and advertising rivalry results indicate a leader versus follower type of non-price competition. The analysis points to Merck as the industry leader. This underscores a remark by Scherer that Merck was the industry leader in 1992 (Scherer 1993, 102). In the R&D battle ground, firms show the highest reaction to Merck and smaller reactions to other firms. In the advertising arena, the most significant reactions again point to Merck as the leader.

Firm Size, and Innovation through a Total Factor Productivity Model

Hypothesis 3 addresses rivalry through an environment in which the size of a firm influences its innovative activities. The model we identified above was intensively measured by Mansfield (1980, 1983, 1988) at the firm, industry, and country levels. We have adopted the model for our firm size versus innovation hypothesis. It requires us to use some different measures of the data. We have used the S&P definition for total capital and employment, sales as a proxy for Q, and, following Mansfield, R&D as a measure of innovation. The traditional use of the model is

Table 6.4   SUR regressions of firms advertising outlays on rivals

Dep./Ind.	Constant	Rival's R&D (–1)	Own patent (–1)	R^2	DW
Abbott/Merck	0.92 (2.93)***	0.55 (3.29)***	0.15 (1.05)	0.98	0.59
American/Merck	3.76 (11.98)***	0.23 (3.72)***	0.17 (2.08)**	0.92	0.06
Bristol/Merck	3.55 (19.25)***	0.37 (5.75)***	0.21 (5.41)***	0.95	1.19
Lilly/Merck	7.54 (14.01)***	0.03 (0.22)	–0.62 (–4.44)***	0.69	1.79
Johnson/Merck	1.47 (4.84)***	0.37 (4.15)***	0.40 (4.98)***	0.92	1.55
Pfizer/Merck	3.24 (9.10)***	0.78 (9.11)***	–0.28 (–3.00)***	0.87	1.35
Abbott/Pfizer	1.50 (2.29)**	0.30 (1.47)	0.24 (2.42)***	0.77	0.39
American/Pfizer	2.64 (10.09)***	–0.13 (–0.77)	0.61 (4.23)***	0.92	2.00
Bristol/Pfizer	3.39 (21.03)***	0.39 (11.27)***	0.21 (6.52)***	0.96	0.57
Lilly/Pfizer	6.15 (9.43)***	–0.40 (–1.24)	–0.07 (00.29)	0.58	1.22
Johnson/Pfizer	1.48 (6.45)***	0.32 (5.66)***	0.42 (7.00)***	0.96	1.34
Merck/Pfizer	3.23 (3.00)***	–0.22 (–0.66)	0.42 (2.74)***	0.54	0.21
American/Abbott	4.13 (9.48)***	0.40 (3.65)***	0.03 (0.24)	0.88	1.48
Bristol/Abbott	3.77 (16.75)***	0.27 (3.16)***	0.27 (6.05)***	0.93	1.14
Lil (ly/Abbott	6.96 (13.06)***	0.18 (1.16)	–0.63 (–4.57)***	0.68	1.67
Johnsn/Abbott	1.61 (5.21)***	0.41 (3.97)***	0.38 (4.96)****	0.92	1.84
Merck/Abbott	0.60 (1.97)**	1.06 (7.83)***	–0.06 (–0.60)	0.94	1.47
Pfizer/Abbott	3.01 (7.81)***	0.50 (4.71)***	–0.01 (–0.08)	0.84	1.24
Abbott/American	–1.58 (–1.25)	0.78 (2.81)***	0.23 (2.70)***	0.83	0.63
Bristol/American	0.98 (1.25)	0.74 (4.41)***	0.19 (4.14)****	0.91	0.56
Lilly/American	6.88 (5.05)***	–0.002 (–0.01)	–0.49 (–3.65)***	0.69	1.74
Johnson/American	–0.93 (–1.28)	0.60 (3.48)***	0.49 (7.69)***	0.93	1.89
Merck/American	–0.52 (–0.28)	0.53 (1.25)	0.34 (2.66)***	0.76	0.26
Pfizer/American	–0.76 (–0.95)	0.95 (4.80)***	0.04 (0.44)	0.84	0.59
Abbott/Bristol	–0.10 (–0.09)	0.15 (0.47)	0.57 (3.21)***	0.89	0.92
American/Bristol	2.97 (11.57)***	–0.17 (–0.76)	0.64 (2.99)***	0.93	2.00
Lilly/Bristol	6.74 (7.50)***	–0.01 (–0.02)	–0.46 (–1.74)*	0.69	1.69
Johnson/Bristol	–0.38 (–1.02)	0.66 (6.30)***	0.30 (4.45)***	0.96	1.15
Merck/Bristol	–2.63 (–2.05)**	0.76 (2.15)**	0.37 (1.95)**	0.84	0.58
Pfizer/Bristol	–4.95 (–4.44)***	2.10 (6.53)***	–0.57 (–2.58)***	0.77	0.25
Abbott/Johnson	–0.53 (–0.62)	0.87 (3.24)***	–0.01 (–0.05)	0.77	0.55
Amer./Johnson	3.38 (14.03)***	0.77 (7.06)***	–0.27 (–2.75)***	0.89	1.69
Bristol/Johnson	2.09 (7.89)***	0.70 (7.10)***	0.08 (1.17)	0.95	0.87
Lilly/Johnson	6.58 (8.67)***	0.69 (2.59)***	–1.07 (–5.48)***	0.60	1.88
Merck/Johnson	–0.98 (–0.93)	0.98 (2.78)***	0.02 (0.11)	0.79	0.44
Pfizer/Johnson	–2.20 (–3.58)***	1.45 (6.31)***	–0.17 (–0.88)	0.89	0.48
Abbott/Lilly	6.17 (4.54)***	–0.30 (–1.09)	–0.06 (–0.72)	0.03	0.19
American/Lilly	5.89 (9.95)***	–0.18 (–1.98)**	0.13 (2.57)***	0.65	0.64
Bristol/Lilly	2.49 (3.93)***	0.39 (3.40)***	0.44 (10.71)***	0.83	0.33
Johnson/Lilly	3.12 (3.19)***	–0.18 (–1.28)	0.52 (6.83)***	0.81	1.58
Merck/Lilly	12.94 (5.51)***	–1.11 (–2.40)***	–0.55 (–3.94)***	–0.62	0.19
Pfizer/Lilly	7.57 (6.29)***	–0.21 (–0.87)	–0.23 (–2.57)**	–0.43	0.22

Note: All variables are in logarithmic form. Numbers in brackets are t-values. Three asterisks represent significance at the 99% level; two, significance at the 95% level, and one, significance at the 90% level.

to regress TFP against time to obtain an estimate of its growth rate, λ, or against R&D to obtain the influence of R&D on TFP. Instead, we use it in our rivalry equations above to ascertain rivalry. In the table, we indicate with an "x" only regression equations with significant reaction coefficients of the proper signs. To fit the equations for each firm, we experimented with a variety of techniques such as SUR and 3SLQ, and several specifications such as Cobb-Douglas and CES. The best fits were associated with three-stage least squares, using the log values of the firms' patents as instruments. The results are as follows:

Table 6.5   Regression estimates 3SLQ, production functions for firms, 1980–1999

Dependent variable: sales/labor	Constant	Capital/labor	R&D/labor	R^2
	2.67	0.23	0.51	
Abbott	(12.78)***	(3.74)***	(15.45)	0.98
	5.12	−0.43	0.78	
American	(19.50)***	(−4.50)***	(10.41)***	0.97
	−0.15	1.23	−0.12	
Bristol	(−0.17)	(4.63)***	(−0.76)	0.94
	1.24	0.84	0.02	
Johnson	(4.93)***	(7.69)***	(0.24)	0.98
	2.14	0.39	0.33	
Lilly	(3.49)***	(1.87)*	(2.32)***	0.94
	0.81	0.61	0.47	
Merck	(3.00)***	(6.12)***	(3.64)***	0.95
	3.28	0.09	0.49	
Pfizer	(18.86)***	(1.76)*	(21.65)***	0.99

The results for the first phase of the calculations in Table 6.5 indicate that the R&D variables are significant for Abbott, and Bristol. All the capital coefficients are significant, and only one intercept term, for Bristol, is insignificant. We use these results to calculate the TFP, insert these values into EQ1 for R&D, and then proceed to estimate the second phase of the analysis. Because we estimate only nine of 42 TFP reaction coefficients, we qualitatively discuss the results via a grid.

Leading firms:	Reacting firms to leaders TFP in the previous period			
	Pfizer	Abbott	Bristol	Merck
Abbott	x		x	x
American	x		x	
Bristol	x	x		
Johnson	x			
Lilly		x		

We note that Pfizer reacts in its TFP rivalry to all the firms excepting Merck and Lilly, Abbott reacts to Bristol and Lilly, Bristol reacts to Abbott and American, and Merck reacts only to Abbott. The notable feature of the grid is that Pfizer and Merck are absent from the leading role in TFP rivalry, and Pfizer is a strong reactor to small firms TFP. Along with the one instance of Merck reaction to Abbott, we lean towards the conclusion that a large firm shows a significant reaction to a small firm in TFP.

From the above observations we lean towards the conclusion that small firms are leaders in total factor productivity rivalry; at the very least, large firms do not have a TFP advantage over small firms. This is reminiscent of the Kefauver Committee argument that innovation is not necessarily occurring within the firms, but is instead occurring outside of the industry (Comanor 1986, 1189). An alternative explanation as to why the large firms react to small firms is because small firms are most likely to seize the opportunity to develop a new molecular rather than a new chemical entity. According to a USDC study, "As soon as a new chemical compound with useful physiological activity is discovered and patented by a pharmaceutical company, numerous competitors try to improve it by finding a new patentable chemical variant through molecular manipulation" (USDC 1984, 11). This conclusion is also at the heart of the Kamien and Schwartz (1975, 15) conclusion that non-price competition is "primarily a tool of small firms seeking profit improvement by introducing new substitutes for the existing product." Therefore, it would be in the interest of large firms to monitor the small firms' TFP activities closely.

In sum, while we found that Merck is a viable leader in R&D and advertising separately, we find that large firms have a tendency to follow small firm's activities when TFP is the rivalry weapon. The fact that a firm's capital and labor are behind the calculation of TFP may account for the differences in the two divergent conclusions. However, the drive to get a NME rather than a NCE is more in the province of the smaller firms that are more likely to be strapped for cashflow and behind in their patent awards. We recognize the need for better measures of R&D capital, NCE instead of sales, and perhaps a separation of basic from applied research. Improved data is required to further investigate these conclusions. However, at this point we observe that the size versus innovation hypothesis holds out a contrary possibility for the large versus small firm rivalry hypothesis that exists under the R&D and advertising hypothesis.

Conclusion

In this chapter, we investigated a broad array of hypotheses related to the pharmaceutical industry. For the globalization period, we find that R&D is a focal variable that is supplemented with detailing and sales promotion activities. Although R&D is considered a nonrivalrous good from the "endogenous growth" model viewpoint, firms do compete with respect to outlays as they are showing willingness to cooperate with the government on the other. We found that the seven firms we investigated over the 1980–1999 period react to each other in their R&D and advertising outlays. We found leadership-follower patterns, where the other six firms react to Merck's previous period outlay of R&D and advertising, given the state of their patent awards and cash flow, respectively. We arrived at these results using traditional models in the literature with careful econometric specification and specialization to the pharmaceutical industry. To our knowledge, the mere finding of rivalry reaction patterns is here investigated for the first time in the literature. The focal concern of firms on R&D in this industry justifies making it the primary sector from the "endogenous growth" model viewpoint. It confirms the belief that the pharmaceutical industry may have traditional structural patterns, despite its reputation of being concentrated in R&D and patent activities.

Our results also found that rivalry in regards to TFP does not honor large firm dominance over small firms. As noted above, this touches on an old concern of the Kefauver Committee investigation that most new discoveries take their source from outside the industry. Because of their disadvantage in size, we have suggested that an explanation for this behavioral pattern is anchored in small firms' likelihood to look for NMEs rather than for NCEs. Small firms are most apt to copy an industry technology, for instance by being aggressive to create a new molecular entity. This is their way to make inroads into the larger firm shares. Such activities over time are captured in the TFP measure, of which we find that large firms are mindful.[1]

---

[1] The firms' financial data is from the S&P 500 Stock Market Encyclopedia and Compustat. Industry R&D is taken from Pharmaceutical Research and Manufacturers of America (PhRMA Annual Survey, 2001, 117). Patent data is taken from the United States Patent & Trademark Office, Patent Full Text and Image Database (http://www.uspto.gov/patft/index.html). Advertising data represents the cost of advertising media (radio, television, newspapers, and periodicals) and promotional expenses, and excludes selling and marketing expenses. Compustat has another series entitled selling, general and administrative expenses, which we did not use because it included R&D expenditures whose influence we are separating from advertising. For the TFP hypothesis, we used S&P's employment and total capital data.

Chapter 7

The Printing and Publishing Industry

Introduction

Within a global framework, we examine how the US printing and publishing industry (PPI) structure bends and fits within the new high-tech environment. We calculate trade coefficients to capture its performance and responses with the relevant trade regime it operates. Our investigation from a CGE point of view shows that the industry uses more resources than before. We begin with a survey of the changing structure of the industry, and follow by estimating the net benefits from trade adjustments.

The US printing and publishing industry is essential to the enhancement and dissemination of knowledge in the current environment of Information Technology (IT) advancements and global economic changes. These adjustments in this industry's global and IT environments have important implications for its market structure. In order to grasp the transitional nature of the industry's structure, we need to delineate its traditional features for comparison. PPI is traditionally viewed as having relatively low concentration and labor-intensive technology. As well, smaller firms traditionally contract larger firms for printing and distribution. Profitability depends on book sales volume, and few firms are profitable. The majority of distribution is through retail and college stores, libraries and institutions, schools and most recently mail orders, particularly through the Internet (S&P *Industry Survey* 1985, M89).

The growth of the IT sector and the subsequent changes in copyright and contractual licensing laws have upset the traditional industry structure. According to Varian, we can infer that the IT sector has influenced economic categories such as product and price differentiation, search, bundling, switching cost and lock-in, economies of scale from demand and supply sides, standards, system effects, and computer mediated transactions (Varian 2001, 65–102). For instance, an Association of American Publishers, Inc, (AAP) report states that the internet has made it possible for anyone to publish, and that "contractual licensing—particularly through the use of "clickscreens" and other standard form agreements—contributes to the elimination of entry barriers" (AAP 2002, 9).

The impact of IT advances on copyright and licensing laws in the PPI suggest that increased concentration and competition can coexist. While there are many booksellers (about 30,000) in the United States retail book market, few sell books through the Internet. Before the Internet, a local bookstore had a degree of market power, as customers tended to patronize the local stores. But while only a few booksellers monopolize the Internet (such as Amazon), prices are significantly lower. The apparent paradox can be explained with the new IT paradigm; consumers search the internet easily for the best buy amongst the few vendors, a practice unavailable within the traditional distribution channels. For instance, Brynjolfsson (2001, 106) found that search costs on the Internet save about 30 times more than the cost from a phone call, and about 30 times more than the "shoe-leather" cost of visiting a store.

The influence of IT and regulation on the bookseller's structure also has negative side effects for the industry. As Gordon pointed out: "Barnes and Noble and Borders would have been content to play a dominant role in the retailing of books, but were forced by competition from Amazon.com to become 'clicks and mortar'... taking customers, profits, or capital gains away from other companies. This is a zero-sum game" (Gordon 2000, 69). Similarly, we find that "Sales of printed versions of all encyclopedias, including Britannica, collapsed by over 80 per cent in the 1990s, as the content was bundled for 'free' with office software or delivered on the web" (Brynjolfsson and Hitt 2000, 43).

In the technology-based scenario, the role of international trade has shown a partiality for positive net trade. Exports and licensing rights to US books, for example, have grown at rate greater than the US book market and thus attract increased attention from United States publishers (*US Outlook* 1999, 25–2). "(P)ublishing generates far more exports than imports, making a significant and positive contribution to the net trade balance" (AAP, 6). The drive towards trade liberalization under the Uruguay round of GATT has protected copyrights and lowered or eliminated tariffs on many printed products, thus it should enhance the growth trends. In the same vein, the World Intellectual Property Organization (WIPO) copyright treaties in 101 nations, including the United States, will enhance exports. The new environment, therefore, makes direct exports and international joint ventures more attractive for United States publishers (*US Outlook* 2000, 25–3). No doubt, technological change and licensing are cooperating in the global scene to drive the export growth.

Digital technology has also changed the traditional separation between e-books and print-on-demand choices that are the special services provided by the modern technology. While this new technology is still at the infant stage of development, we note the trend in the industry to limit to publishing and stockpiling before selling, which is particularly advantageous at the international level.

While the significant licensing and IT changes continue, no comprehensive analysis exists to assess the industry structure. The few studies on the book publishing segment of the industry (Machlup 1977, Curwen 1977, Szenberg and Lee 1990, 1994, Bittlingmayer 1988, 1992) do not include a global and IT review of the industry; such analysis is limited to reports in the trade and literature. Our objective is to fill the gap. The next section develops a Computation General Equilibrium (CGE) model to examine United States competitiveness in the PPI and to capture the retailing licensing trends of the industry.

Models

The model we use is based on the Heckscher-Ohlin theory, as modified by Craft and Thomas (1986). Although Baldwin (1971) has explored the Net Export (Export – Import) by labor force and various indices for scale, union and concentration, and factor intensity, he is on record stating that "… if one is interested in the best indicator of export performance (as they are), a variable including imports is not appropriate" (Baldwin 1972). Because a new data set is available for exports, it is worthwhile to look at it from the PPI's point of view to examine if differences in sign and level of coefficients are not different from the two-factor studies of Baldwin (1971), Craft and Thomas (1986), and Wright (1990). Within that broad export framework, we will inevitably trespass on the grounds of other related hypotheses, which we list as follows:

> **Hypothesis 1 (Balassa 1979)**: *There are stages of comparative advantage. Developed countries tend to export goods that are capital intensive, including human capital, and import unskilled labor intensive goods.*

> **Corollary to Hypothesis 1 (Krugman 1994)**: *Developed countries export highly capital-intensive goods, such as airplanes, for which they benefit from economies of scale.*

> **Hypothesis 2 (Craft and Thomas 1986, 631)**: *Cross-section models among all industries are difficult to specify for natural resource-intensive products because of climate, ecology, and geological differences across trading nations.*

> **Corollary to Hypothesis 2 (Wright 1990)**: *Simple mind models are not applicable to trade in more than one factor cases.*

For econometric specification, we need to examine the trade section of a country's balance sheet. We start from the premise that the balance of payment (BOP) is in equilibrium when the Current Account (CA) and Capital Account (KA) plus official reserves are in tandem. In symbolic form:

$$CA + KA + \text{Reserves} = BOP \qquad \text{Eq. 1}$$

Commodity exports such as printing and publishing affect the CA side of the BOP. The CA can be recast into identities that bring out the hypotheses above. For instance, CA can be expressed as the interest on foreign assets plus net exports, or through other financial identities such as a combination of FDI, foreign and other investment portfolios, and reserves. In the backdrop of the Heckscher-Ohlin model, and with the aid of such identities, one can formulate a specification in line with Baldwin (1971), Craft and Thomas (1986), and Wright (1990) as follows:

Net trade =
f(Factor Intensity, Human Capital, and Dummies for sample influences such
as NAFTA)   Eq. 2

It has been stated that the PPI has been a net positive contributor to the trade
account, i.e., export – import is positive. This may be negated by deficits in the
accounts of other industries, such as textiles and apparel, steel, and automobiles.
The above industries were devastated during the trade liberalization periods of
various free trade areas (FTAs) agreements with Canada, Israel, and North
America. Along with lower tariffs and rivalry from EMU, the NAFTA countries
have been following a policy that made capital more mobile. That has made the
interplay between CA and KA more difficult to predict, as when capital mobile
currency crisis may be perpetuated through misuse of capital and its influence
on the exchange rates through diminishing reserves. As liberalization expands
globally, financial crises have been erupting among the Asian and NAFTA
countries, such as Mexico. It is important to understand the PPI point of view.
It is also important to perform an empirical assessment of the PPI's performance
through an investigation of growth variables in that period. Schwartzman (1969,
1971) uses sales per labor ratio cum sales per output and output per labor ratio,
$S/H = S/O \times O/H$, to assess the performance of the retail sector over the long run.
In this production function setting, factors' contribution alongside utilization of
capacity and economies of scale have indicated a long-term decline in performance
in sales to the extent of –0.21 (Schwartzman 1969, 204). Our emphasis, however,
is to examine within a short time frame how the IT and the global sector play
out their influences on the PPI.

Empirical Results

We perform two kinds of empirical investigations. First, we investigate overall
patterns of trade based on the model. Then we estimate the welfare benefits for
the industry in the global economy based on the liberalization of tariffs and TAA
benefits for the NAFTA.

Trade Patterns for the PPI

The United States PPI competes on a global scale with greater vigor than other
industries. Table 7.1 reports its share relative to the world trade from 1970 to
1998. Both the United States' and NAFTA regions' share of exports declined,
respectively, from their high of 16.1 and 34.4 per cent in 1970 to 11.9 and 21.8 per
cent in 1990. However, the year of NAFTA, 1994, saw a reversal of that trend,
reaching up to 14.8 and 27.4 per cent, respectively, in 1998. The indication is that
trade liberalization was at work for the industry.

Table 7.1   Historic trade trends (in thousands of dollars), paper and publishing products, 1970–1998

	1970	%	1980	%	1990	%	1994	%	1998	%
Sectors										
US	1,192	16.09	5,245	13.93	10,526	11.88	17,714	14.78	14,191	13.00
Canada	1,328		4,504		8,538		14,214		14,945	
Mexico	26		129		273		610	648		
NAFTA	2,546	34.36	9,878	26.24	19,337	21.82	32,538	27.16	29,784	27.4
World	7,410		37,649		88,636		119,817		108,832	

Source: Compiled from GTAP 5 Time Series Data Base.

Table 7.2 displays regression results that explain GTAP's export data within the modified factor abundant theories of Baldwin (1971), Craft and Thomas (1986), and Wright (1990) discussed above. Column 1 indicates that all the coefficients are significant at the 99 per cent confidence level. The adjusted R^2 is particularly high at 0.91, and the Durbin Watson statistics do not even reach level 2, implying a chance for some negative serial correlation. The novelty of including Trade Adjustment Assistance along with factor intensity, human capital, and NAFTA has paid off. When workers are displaced from trade liberalization, exports suffer. The influence is less significant for FTAs besides NAFTA, as indicated in Column 2.

The negative capital intensity coefficient of Table 7.2 continues to underscore the strong complementarities between certain natural resources and physical capital (Baldwin 1971, 142). The historic approach of Wright (1990, 659) indicates that the capital/labor ratio was positive until 1940, when a natural resource variable is included, but then it started turning negative again, underscoring Baldwin's (1971) results. In the timeframe that we have considered, the result is perhaps reflective of the fact that when trade barriers were removed through liberalization policies, the United States received natural resources from abroad.

Table 7.2 indicates that the human capital coefficient is positive, underscoring our expectation that the US is an exporter of human capital within the timeframe of our investigation. This is due in large part to the influence of the IT sector. This result, coupled with the negative capital/labor ratio, indicates that technology in the PPI is being used more as a resource. Columns 3 and 4 repeat the analysis for net exports.

Table 7.2   Regression results, selected economic characteristics, printing and publishing industry, 1987–1998

	Column 1 GTAP trade data	Column 2 GTAP trade data
Constant	−22.78 (−2.47)***	−43.90 (−4.97)***
Capital/labor	−0.005 (−3.65)***	−0.003 (−1.83)
Trade adjustment assistance	−4.71 (−4.23)***	−2.64 (−1.96)*
Human capital	2.7 x 10^5 (5.89)***	3.4x10^5 (5.96)***
NAFTA	5.91 (3.09)***	
Adj. R^2	0.91	0.87
DW	2.22	2.06
Sample	1987–1998	1987–1998

Note: Trade adjustment assistance is measured by the number of employees (certified and denied) TAA. Human capital = hourly wage rate/hours worked. NAFTA = Dummy variable = 1 since 1994. Three asterisks indicate 99 %. Confidence level (CL); Two refer to 95%. CL; One refers to 90%. CL. Items in parentheses are t-values.

Computation General Equilibrium Results

Table 7.3 assesses the level of benefits to the United States and NAFTA in terms of welfare benefits to consumers. The results of Part I illustrate the profit levels for 1997, approximately four years after the NAFTA negotiations. The profit for 1997 to the US was $12.24 billion following scheduled tariff reduction. Should the world reduce tariffs by 10 per cent on all goods, column 3 would indicate that profits to the US could increase to $13.38 billion. Should tariffs be completely eliminated the US benefits could increase to $23.32 billion. Finally, should the tariff reduction affect only the PPI sector for all countries the US benefits could be $12.61 billion.

All through the liberalization scenarios for 1997 world benefits would be increasing from its base year of 1997 implied tariff structure. The actual increase would be from $62.59 billion with the implied tariff structure, to $65.28 for 10 per cent liberalization, to $76.91 for complete liberalization, and to $62, 628 billion if only the PPI sector was liberalized. Of course, the benefit to liberalization is mingled with improved international copyright laws that were boosted under the Uruguay round of negotiations. But the CGE model indicates that the magic of liberalization has a demonstrated positive comparative static result, indicating increased benefits from liberalization.

In order to compare 1997 results with other years, we have completed the simulation with the 1995 GTAP database. The results are in Part 1a of Table 7.3. Comparing the top rows of Part 1 with Part 1a, we observe that the benefits to the US were consistently lower in 1997 than in 1995, as recorded in Columns 1–5. The underlying theory is that although liberalization will enhance benefits, other forces in the economy have been adversely affecting the sector over the three-year period from 1995–1997. According to a reputable report "the 'disappearing boundaries' in book publishing are the literal boundaries between nations of the world" (*Book Industry Study Group* 2000, 6). Also, disappearing is the distinction between "books, and book-related products and services" (ibid., 4). The results are as follows: companies such as Barnes and Noble and Random House venture into non-traditional areas such as e-publishing, wholesalers and distributors venture into digitalized distribution networks, and authors are concerned with shifting from primary rights such as printing, publishing, and selling into secondary rights such as audio, film, or TV rights. Within that milieu of changes, the economic measure of publisher's sales for the industry witnessed a drop in sales on all books in 1996. From 1993, the sales increased from \$17,680.9 in 1994 to \$17,733.2 in 1995, but fell to \$17,639 in 1996 (ibid., 184).

Part 2 of Table 7.3 assesses the benefits from imitation or rivalry from other free trade areas of the world. According to a Gale Research study (1996, 682), NAFTA "was expected to lead to significant growth in the US book trade with Mexico, and other Latin American markets in the 1990s." Similarly, the Uruguay Round enhanced protection for international copyrights, which was expected to lead to a larger market for international publishers in Asia, the Middle East, and Eastern Europe. In Latin America, Africa, and Asia publishers have reached widely different degrees of business and technical sophistication. We have therefore disaggregated the trading blocks and commodities to ascertain the various shares of these regions, and also to consider what the effect of trade distortion will have on benefits. Comparing the first row of Parts 1 and 2, we find that the US share is not significantly distorted in the disaggregated module. Column 2 versus 7 puts the loss at \$75 million, Column 3 versus 8, \$355 million, Column 4 versus 9, \$617 million, and Columns 5 versus 10, –\$252 million, with the average loss being \$15.75 million. Although the United States is in stiff competition with the world, its share has been very stable between the highly aggregated model of Part 1 and the aggregated model of Part 2.

Gross, and TAA benefits should be adjusted for transfer payments such as relocation expenses. Since 1962, the Department of Labor has offered TAA benefits to compensate workers for import displacement costs, and to enhance occupational and geographical mobility. Under the strict law of its early phase,

Table 7.3   CGE welfare benefits under various tariff cut scenarios, domestic import elasticity = 2, foreign = 4, 1995 and 1997, in billions of dollars

1) 4×2: Countries by PPI and others (1997)

Regions of countries	Benefits without tariff cuts ($billion)	Benefits with all tariff cuts=10%	Benefits complete liberalization	Liberalizing only PPI for all countries
Col. 1	Col. 2	Col. 3	Col. 4	Col. 5
US	$12.240	$13.380	$23.324	$12.612
CAN	$1.964	$1.915	$1.737	$1.927
MEX	$1.928	$1.772	$0.071	$1.972
NAFTA	$16.132	$17.066	$25.131	$16.511
ROW	$46.457	$48.209	$51.779	$46.117
World	$62.590	$65.275	$76.909	$62.628
1a) 4×2: Countries by PPI and others (1995				
US	$21.407	$23.814	$46.832	$21.761
CAN	$0.682	$0.560	–$0.719	$0.677
MEX	$0.752	$0.669	–$0.437	$0.747
NAFTA	$22.841	$25.043	$45.676	$23.185
ROW	$32.480	$33.928	$31.359	$32.320
World	$55.321	$58.971	$77.034	$55.504

2) 9×10: 9 countries by 10 sectors (1997)

Regions of countries	Benefits without tariff cuts ($billion)	Benefits with all tariff cuts=10%	Benefits: complete liberalization	Liberalizing only PPI for all countries
Col. 6	Col. 7	Col. 8	Col. 9	Col. 10
US	$12.165	$13.025	$23.941	$12.360
CAN	$1.201	$1.314	$4.309	$1.162
MEX	$1.529	$1.470	$0.093	$1.527
NAFTA	$14.895	$15.809	$28.343	$15.049
EUR	$17.144	$18.338	$18.603	$17.591
ASP	$20.840	$25.518	$53.141	$20.925
FSU	$1.443	$1.462	$0.890	$1.399
AFR	$0.808	$1.010	$0.494	$0.687
LAC	$0.625	$1.262	$6.553	$0.497
ROW	$0.398	$0.577	$1.806	$0.357
World	$56.153	$63.976	$109.831	$56.506

Note: Assumptions: CES of capital and labor; CET between domestic and exported goods, and CES for the final demand of the single, representative consumer. Sluggish land and natural resources, and mobile capital, and skill and unskilled labor. Column 3: the world is liberalized 10%. Column 4: complete liberalization of the world—tax multiplier = 0. Column 5: Only PPI sector is liberalized for the US. The 10 sectors for Part 2 are: steel, publishing and printing, chemical, food, machinery, metals, motor vehicles, textiles, wearing apparel, and others.

however, only a few workers qualified, but the requirements became easier during the 1980s and 1990s. Table 7.4 indicates how the certification and denial process of TAA operated from 1980–1999. Although the number of petitions was small, the number of employees affected totaled in the thousands. In the PPI 4,028 employees were certified, and 8,147 were denied during the 1980–1999 period.

We notice that after every FTA, the number of petitions and, therefore, the number of workers affected is larger than during non-FTA periods. The implication is, as expected, that the industry suffered from free competition. The distinction between per cent certified and denied in the pre and post FTA periods does not tell a compelling story. For instance, it is hard to argue that the percentage of petitions denied after a liberalization effort has dropped.

FTA agreements do not lead to a lower denial percentage in TAA benefits. Only after NAFTA, did the percentage of employees denied TAA benefits decrease from 9.53 to 6.39 per cent. In all other instances this number remains constant. Perhaps the affected number of employees is large relative to the industry, i.e., it does not loom large in the nation's employment or political agenda. Perhaps also, as Szenberg and Lee (1994) have argued, the book industry in particular is a "for-profit" business, letting the private sector primarily absorb the shock. Governmental factors are important, but so are also a host of other factors including: the number and budgets of libraries, political instability, birth rates, education, living standards, labor costs, cultural traditions, and available leisure time (Gale Research 1996, 681). The only notable regulatory reform in this industry has been the recent January 2002 No Child Left Behind Act (NCLB), which has the potential to stimulate the demand side of the industry. Otherwise, the private sector prevails.

Table 7.5 indicates our estimate of the benefits from TAA for this industry. It shows trade liberalization benefits in the first section and TAA costs in the second section. The cost of TAA is not larger for this industry. In perpetuity (PV=1/r), trade liberalization confers benefits to the extent of $1,591 billion with a 1995 base estimate of $21.4 billion, declining to $909 billion in 1997 with a $12.2 billion base. The cost in perpetuity of TAA, about half the costs to a footwear worker, is at $.52 and $.24 billion, respectively.

Conclusion

The paper and printing industry has been opened up to international competition from trade liberalization efforts in the areas of IT and regulation. The PPI structure examined within a modified H-O two factor model predicts consistently with the hypotheses of Baldwin (1971), Craft and Thomas (1986), and Wright (1990). The factor intensity coefficient is significant and negative, implying complementarities between capital and natural resource factors in trade. Along with the positive human capital influence of the PPI, we have an indication that the PPI structure is using more resources.

Table 7.4   Petitions and employment experience in the PPI, 1980–1999

	Petitions				Employment			
	Total certified	Total denied	Annual % certified	Annual % denied	Total certified	Total denied	Annual % certified	Annual % denied
1980–1999	32	86			4028	8147		
NAFTA:								
1980–1993	12	36	2.68%	2.99%	1341	4505	2.38%	3.95%
1994–1999	20	50	8.93%	8.31%	2687	3642	9.53%	6.39%
ISFTA								
1980–1986	2	4	0.89%	0.66%	116	131	0.41%	0.23%
1987–1999	30	82	7.21%	7.33%	3912	8016	7.47%	7.57%
USCAFTA								
1980–1984	1	4	0.63%	0.93%	3	131	0.01%	0.32%
1985–1999	31	82	6.46%	6.36%	4025	8016	6.66%	6.56%

Table 7.5   Cost and benefits estimates for the PPI

Time	PV 1995	Benefits 1997	Average	PV 1995	Costs 1997	Net 1995	Benefits 1997
Value:	21.407	12.24	16.82	0.0072	0.0033	21.40	12.24
Present value for 5 years:							
1	21.12	12.08	16.60	0.0071	0.0032	21.12	12.07
2	20.84	11.92	16.38	0.0070	0.0032	20.84	11.91
3	20.57	11.76	16.16	0.0069	0.0031	20.56	11.76
4	20.29	11.60	15.95	0.0069	0.0031	20.29	11.60
5	20.02	11.45	15.74	0.0068	0.0030	20.02	11.45
Total PV	1591.17	909.79	1250.48	0.5375	0.2419	1590.64	909.55

Note: Assume potential growth of the United States economy at 4% and a discount factor of 6.33%.

On the trade liberalization and worker displacement sides, we find that consumer surplus has been approximately $12 billion in 1997, given the existing level of liberalization at that time. The benefits appear to be substantially smaller than that of 1995, when the major liberalization effort with NAFTA began. The drop is marked by a recognizable fall in value of shipments in 1996. TAA assistance appears too small to create a significant impact in total benefits, unlike the cases of other trade impacted industries such as the footwear, garment, and steel. However, while TAA benefits may appear slight, the number of displaced workers applying for TAA has a significant influence on exports of PPI. As the regression results of Table 7.2 show, the influence is larger because of the advent of NAFTA.

Chapter 8

The Automobile Industry

Introduction

The auto industry fits in neatly with the new trade model within the global economy. Its market structure is characterized as a differentiated oligopoly with non-price competition and price collusion. Non-price competition is mainly along the level of expenditures in advertising and R&D, and the number of dealership franchises. The firms in this industry engage in dealership rivalry partly to maintain the product preferences of buyers, partly to sell a substantial part of their products through retail dealerships, and partly to promote sales, specialized maintenance, repair services, and easy access to replacement parts. Firms can be efficient in the sense that they can reach optimal outcomes because a firm will most likely follow optimal policies at each stage regarding decisions on price collusion, reaction functions for advertising, research and development, and dealership franchise.

Product differentiation and brand loyalty maintained by advertising outlays and enhanced by other non-price weapons allow the firms to price above marginal cost. This should give the government a reason for intervening when foreign firms exact too much rent from the United States according to the propositions of the new trade theories. On the other hand, vertical integration may allow sufficient consumer surplus to be extracted from the parts market to reduce prices to a low level represented by incremental costs, and allows the firms to carry excess capacity. Regarding advertising, firms tend to show strong reactions toward each other's outlays. Even when retailers advertise, either because they have unadvertised brands, excess inventory, or dual brands, rival dealers may not react as one dealer's advertising may sufficiently increase traffic which spill over to the other. At the R&D end, firms are always conducting research to come up with new engineering feats each year.

The troubles for the United States auto industry began in the 1970s, when OPEC raised the price of oil and foreign companies with smaller and fuel efficient cars became more attractive. The United States firms, then four major ones (General Motors, Ford Corporation, Chrysler and American Motors) witnessed foreign producers making great inroads into their domestic market share, which did not stabilize until the mid 1980s. When the first round of OPEC struck in 1973–1974, the share of GM was approximately 44 per cent, Ford's, 24 per cent, and Chrysler and the import's, 16 per cent, as Table 8.1 indicates. During one decade the share of imports increased to approximately 28 per cent by 1983.

Table 8.1   New car market share since OPEC (in %)

Year	GM	Ford	Chrysler	Imports	Comment
Average: 1946–1973	45.8	25.0	16.3	5.8	
1973	44.32	23.5	13.3	15.15	OPEC
1974	41.89	24.96	13.56	15.74	
1979	46.42	20.29	9.02	22.70	OPEC
1983	44.01	17.11	9.19	27.54	

Source: 1946–1983, *Automotive News* 1984 *Market Data Book*, 40.

Protection

In 1981, for the first time since World War II, the industry sought protection from the United States government in the form of Voluntary Export Restraints (VER) (Crandall 1987, 271). Under Section 201 of the 1974 Trade Act, the domestic industry was required to show evidence of impact before any form of relief can be extended. They failed to demonstrate that the import impact dominated the impact of recessions (Feenstra 1989, 125).

The fact that the auto industry has a differentiated oligopolistic market structure has led to an indirect method of testing its performance under standard Heckscher-Ohlin (HO) theorem. For instance, in order to assess the effect of Most Favored Nation (MFN) or optimum tariffs, optimum subsidies, or a combination tariff and subsidies on the industry, Dixit used a model with the major premise that "the government can change the outcome of the oligopoly in the favorable direction. Depending on the precise model of industry structure and conduct, all manner of taxes and subsidies on imports, exports, and domestic production can be justified" (Dixit 1989, 141). The way to get around the monumental task of testing HO is to start with a country production function, for which we derive its GNP or dual revenue function, using time series data and regression analysis for a single country over time. The Stolper-Samuelson and Rybczynski theorems implications will be measured by the revenue function, and those are testable propositions (Feenstra 1989, xiii). This model can be applied to the United States and Japan auto trade in 1979–1980, the year before the Voluntary Export Restraints (VER) resulted in a gain of $17 million over MFN tariff (Dixit 1989, 156).

We now examine the effect of VERs in 1981 on the auto industry under imperfect competition. VERs lasted from May 1981 to 1994, the beginning of NAFTA. At the start, Japan's export was limited to 1.68 million cars, in 1984, 1.85 million from 1985 to early 1992, 2.30 million, and in 1992, 1.65 million. Foreign cars produced domestically were excluded from benefit calculations (Berry et al. 1999, 400–401). The net welfare benefits for the period 1986–1990 were $8.341

billion due to VERs: $10.207 due to profits, $13.135 consumer losses due to higher prices, and $11.269 foregone tariff equivalent (ibid., 423).

The strategic trade relationship took a turn after VERs between United States and Japan. Perhaps due to the dictates of Free Trade, both export and FDI (Foreign Direct Investment) strategies cannot coexist for Japan. Since VERs prevented the former, Japan's strategy shifted toward FDI (Co 1997, 93). Co found that FDI from Japan into the United States increased during the VERs period, but there is no compelling reason to think that FDI and exports are either or choices under the Free Trade premises (ibid., 106).

The so called "transplant" activities of Japanese production into the United States accelerated during the Clinton administration. The two countries entered into a "Global Partnership Plan of Action" in 1992, which required Japan to use more United States-made parts. The agreement has done more than create demand for United States products; it breached a relationship between Japanese car and parts suppliers (Averyt and Ramagopal 1999, 45). The United States was able to strengthen this separation even further by the "Automotive Agreement of 1995" which required the use not only of United States but also parts produced in other countries as well.

Globalism versus Regionalism

Competition with imports pressured the United States industry to go global or regional. Globalization means competition, trade, market seeking investments, cost cutting investments, constraint breaking investments, mergers and acquisitions among automakers, mergers and acquisitions among suppliers, and shared technology (Sturgeon and Florida 2004, 50). The OPEC actions in 1973 and 1979 were landmarks that ushered the industry in the direction of smaller and more efficient cars. The United States firms had to react to the successful Japanese model of small inventory, just-in-time parts warehousing, and better organizational architecture. As they lost market share rapidly, they also sought stronger protection. Global competition led to the transplanting of Japanese operations into the United States and the separation of supplies of parts from vehicle manufacturing. Regional and national concerns were emphasized as part of cost cutting ventures. "Green-filed" plant opportunities by Daimler-Chrysler in Tuscaloosa, Alabama, GM in Fremont, California with Toyota, and Suzuki in Ingersoll, Canada allowed the firms to break the constraint of operating under an old assembly line mold. Global, regional, or national objectives require increased needs to share technology, increasing the emphasis on modularity or the ability to use more integrated engineering designs.

A study of the world automobile industry reached the conclusion that the firms should follow a two-stage approach—first globalize, and afterward regionalize (Schlie and Yip 2000, 343). The study examined strategies that are most suited for the global, regional, or national standpoints. A firm may want to optimize globally in order to "seek a worldwide efficient position", and optimize regionally to balance global challenges with local organizational problems (ibid., 344).

The auto industry is today dominated by regional production. Table 8.2 indicates that North America—United States (12,140,610), Canada (2,546,409), and Mexico (1,585,261)—along with Asia-Pacific and Western Europe account for 87.8 per cent of world production. Yet global forces such as demand, supply, technology, and regulation determine the industry's shape today. Demand is dominated by the target markets of China, India, and Indonesia. Supply conditions such as excess capacity of approximately 30 per cent exists in Western Europe, United States, and Japan, which can supply approximately 22 million additional vehicles per year to meet the potential global demand (ibid., 347). This particular strategy fits in well with the imperfect competition theory of the auto industry.

We noted the protective attitude of the United States and Japan earlier. With NAFTA came the "rules of origin." An auto must have a certain value to qualify for Free Trade (tariff) benefits, which was 62.5 per cent of domestic content for the three countries: United States, Canada, and Mexico. This rule acts as a barrier to imports because foreign parts such as the power train of a car, accounts for about 40 per cent of the value of a domestic car, leaving little room for more imports. In this case regionalism is enhanced.

Technological developments such as vehicle platform-sharing, modular design and assemble, information and communication are both facilitating global and regional development (ibid., 348). In addition, rapid strides are being made in the area of hybrid power technology, including electric, battery, or hydro-powered technology that target regulatory and environmental concerns both globally and at the regional level. While GM and Ford have been known for their regional policies, they are now poised to capture "efficiency on a global scale ... GM, for example, has embarked on a course of globalization and integrating its dispersed regional operations since the early 1990s" (ibid., 350).

Table 8.2   Global vehicle production by regions

Regions	Cars 2003	Trucks 2003	Total	Share
N. America	6,772,811	9,499,469	16,272,280	26.25%
Central and S. America	1,779,908	484,028	2,263,936	3.65%
Asia–Pacific	15,429,307	5,998,862	21,428,169	34.56%
Africa	371,850	180,671	552,521	0.89%
Eastern Europe	2,489,181	376,274	2,865,455	4.62%
Western Europe	15,137,481	2,218,781	17,356,262	27.99%
Middle East	975,752	284,164	1,259,916	2.03%
	42,956,290	19,042,249	61,998,539	

Source: Automotive News Market Data Book 2004, 44.

The current state of the efforts to globalize and regionalize is not without drawbacks. It created more low paying jobs in the industry. Jobs have moved from assembly plants that are more streamlined, to supplier plants, expanding the assembler-supplier wage gap from $24.25 to $17.91 in 2000, respectively (Sturgeon and Florida 2004, 55).

TAA and the Auto Industry

"In the early years, 1997–79, most of the certified workers were from the leather, shoe, textile and apparel industries ... In 1980, auto workers accounted for most of the enormous rise in certifications" (U. S. Congress 1987, 26). Table 8.3 indicates that 600,653 workers and 840 petitions were certified for the sample period 1980–1999. The NAFTA period after 1994 does not show a surge in certifications. As discussed in Chapter 2, the period after the initial OPEC crisis to the mid-1980s was marked by an increase in import shares of the new car markets, and it is not surprising to see that the bulk of certifications for this industry concentrated around 1980.

Table 8.3   Petitions and employment experience of various free trade hypotheses, 1980–1999, autos

	Petitions:		Workers:	
Years	Total certified	Total denied	Total certified	Total denied
1980–1999	840	1,447	600,653	332,110
Data for NAFTA comparison				
1980–1993	753	1,373	587,264	323,093
1994–1999	87	74	13,389	9,017

CGE Results

We now turn to the results from general equilibrium analysis. Column I of Table 8.4 shows the existing states of affairs with the world as of 1997 (GTAP 5.4 Data). The United States is the largest gainer, and along with the NAFTA countries, it accounts for approximately a little less than 2/3 of the benefits in the world (17/42).

Column 2 addresses the scenario where only China and Japan were to be fully liberalized in automobile trade. It is well-known that the United States has been trying to gain access to Japan's and China's market. "Passenger autos produced in the United States and registered in Japan totaled 53,462 units in 1998, a decline of 56 per cent from 1997 levels" (USITC May 1999, 74). United States interest in

China's market is sourced to a Memorandum of Understanding (MOU) dated October 10, 1992. In this agreement, China agreed to significantly liberalize key aspects of its import administration, including reduction of trade barriers and the gradual opening of its markets to United States exports (ibid., 74). We therefore, simulate the scenarios of complete liberalization of these two countries.

Tariff rates in China were expected to decline to 25 per cent in 2005 from a high of 63.5 tariff rate on 80 per cent of goods, and 87.5 tariff rate on 100 per cent goods in 2000. In that year also, quotas were to be phased out, and tariffs on auto parts were expected to be around 10 per cent (ITA 2003, 41–42). Although Japanese duties have been waved in Japan since 1978, Japan had a 3 per cent consumption tax on vehicles in April 1997, which was increased to 5 per cent in 2003. Also, there is an annual automobile tax that depends on engine size, and acquisition taxes for automobiles that varies from 3 to 5 per cent according to business or private uses (ITA 2003, 47). Research found that non-tariff barriers "can be neglected at somewhat less cost than can foreign tariffs" (Deardorff and Stern 1985, 548). Column 2 therefore focuses only on the liberalization of the China auto market. The United States will gain slightly by $0.063 billion, from $13.614 to $13.677, while the world's welfare benefits will increase by $0.286 billion, from $42.249 to $42.535.

Column 3 considers the scenario where all but the NAFTA countries liberalized trade in automobile products. The world's benefits will increase over

Table 8.4   CGE results: welfare benefits for the United States auto industry, in $ billion, 1997

	Column 1	Column 2	Column 3
Mod 1: 2×11; GTAP 5.4	**State of the world benefits**	**China 100% liberalized**	**All but NAFTA 100% liberalized**
Australia	1.865	1.869	1.820
China	2.104	1.777	1.711
Japan	10.640	11.063	15.201
India	0.064	0.066	0.035
Canada	2.047	2.049	2.166
United States	13.614	13.677	14.003
Mexico	1.216	1.216	1.384
France	−3.243	−3.217	−3.256
Germany	−0.563	−0.540	−1.332
Great Britain	0.526	0.532	0.437
Italy	2.024	2.029	2.163
ROW	11.955	12.013	11.165
NAFTA	16.878	16.941	17.553
World	42.249	42.535	45.497

column 1, which represent the current state of the world, by $3.248 billion from $42.249 to $45.497, while the United States benefits will increase by $0.386 billion from $13.614 to $14.003.

Conclusion

The United States auto industry was caught off guard during the OPEC crises in the 1970s. Rising import shares have disrupted the industry's traditional competitive pricing policies, and the domestic automakers had to direct non-price competition toward foreign manufacturers.

Trade liberalization has helped the industry to be more cost efficient, while TAA assistance transitioned workers during restructuring periods. Free trade initiatives have transplanted foreign firms onto United States soil, bringing in foreign direct investment. It has allowed firms to reconsider regionalization in the face of more global competition, and made them opt for protections such as Voluntary Export Restraints. CGE welfare benefits computations indicate that the industry is expecting more benefits as developing economies in the world continue to liberalize their auto markets.

Chapter 9

Perspectives on Policies for Distressed Industries

Introduction

Trade adjustment assistance (TAA) is a relatively recent phenomenon with no strong theoretical underpinnings. Especially since the advent of NAFTA in 1994, it has fostered a substantial amount of new interest and studies with a view to assist traditional trade with the handling of adjustment and associated costs. The year 1994 was a milestone that separated the issues between how trade restrictions increase costs to consumers and producers, and the provision of transitory relief for the pending bountiful gains from free trade in the new global economy. In this chapter, we will investigate the two periods, before and after NAFTA, and the policies that are appropriate for distressed industries.

Policies Before NAFTA

The literature in the pre-NAFTA period includes empirical studies dealing with the significant welfare losses due to trade restrictions. Stephen Magee, for example, had suggested that import restrictions cost American consumers some $18.3 billion in 1972 (Magee 1972, 700).

On the legislative policy side, Congress had always recognized that certain segments of the economy could be adversely affected by changing conditions in international trade and had to determine what sort of remedies should be applied whenever injury due to import competition occurred. Prior to the enactment of the Trade Expansion Act (TEA) of 1962, the President's major policy tool was the escape clause under Article XIX of the General Agreement of Tariffs and Trade (GATT), which provided for tariff and/or quota relief. Subsequently, intervening legislation, such as the Trade Agreement Extension Act of 1951 further refined the language of the escape clause and empowered the Tariff Commission to conduct such investigations upon application by representatives of an injured industry (Banner 1966, 1320–33).

The antecedents of adjustment assistance are to be found in numerous legislative proposals of the 1950s but they only achieved policy significance under Title III of the TEA of 1962. David McDonald, President of the United Steelworkers Union, first focused public attention on the issue in 1954, when as a member of the commission on Foreign Economic Policy (Randall Commission), he proposed that import-injured companies, communities, and workers be made eligible to receive government assistance (Bratt 1974, 2–3). The adoption of adjustment assistance in the United States was also inspired by foreign governments' programs, including those related to economic integration in Europe, although only the United States and Canada had programs at that time that specifically tie adjustment assistance to injury (Corden 1974, 111).

The TEA of 1962 was the first piece of American legislation to provide for adjustment assistance to firms and workers injured by import competition. Rather than rely on the escape clause as a remedy to injured industries, the TEA provided for a program of adjustment assistance directly to firms and/or groups of workers, regardless of whether injury was applicable to the respective entities or to the industry as a whole. Firms injured by imports could apply for low-cost federal loans, technical assistance and tax relief, while workers could receive adjustment allowances during a specified period of time, retraining, and relocation grants. In this way, the TEA presented the first opportunity for individual firms and groups of workers to petition for relief on their own, without proof of injury to their respective industry as a whole. Individual assistance, therefore, appeared to be a more realistic approach to the problem than tariff restrictions, since not every firm in a given industry will be adversely affected by imports at the same time. In addition, the disturbing effects of international trade restrictions may be skirted, and consumers at large may score a net gain on several grounds. For one, the prices of imported goods will not rise in the absence of trade restrictions and the range of choices open to consumers may be significantly enlarged. Low-income consumers, in particular, would gain the most, since they are particularly sensitive to price increases and because low-priced goods from abroad are the usual targets of the United States import restrictions.

Experience with adjustment assistance under the TEA has produced mixed results. In the first seven years since its inception (1962–1969) petitioning firms and workers were generally unsuccessful in their attempts to secure assistance. A mere $18.5 million had been authorized for the program by the end of 1972, and only half of this amount was actually allocated (Jaffe and Nagel 1974, 4). In its operative period since 1970, some assistance has in fact been provided to petitioning firms and workers.

A number of reasons have been advanced for this slow start of the program. It may well be that economic units were not aware of the law and, hence, were ignorant of its provisions for assistance. Many Kennedy Rounds tariff reductions actually took place between 1963 and 1972, and it was thus only in 1970–1971 that firms began to feel the real effects of these concessions (Bale 1974, 52). Also, injured parties may have been discouraged by the negative experience of others; and business and labor support for a more liberal trade policy may have weakened (Fook 1972). Last, but not least, a major cause of this apparent inactivity probably lies in the lengthy and complex procedures for determining eligibility and the stringent criteria, which govern same. We now turn to a detailed examination of these criteria, since they are at the heart of the program.

Section 301 of the TEA lists four conditions that must be met before a firm or worker is eligible to apply for adjustment assistance, or an industry is eligible to apply for tariff relief. These conditions are the same as those required for industry wide relief under escape clause action.

1) The import of a product like or directly competitive with an article produced by the petitioning firm (or worker) must be increasing.

This determination has been generally accomplished with not too much difficulty. Once it is established that imported products are substitutes for those produced by the petitioning firm(s) or workers, it is sufficient to observe whether imports have increased over time. In making this determination, the Tariff Commission usually considers only absolute increases in import levels and requires that an imported item show a definite upward trend. At times, however, the Commission has also considered the ratio of imports to domestic consumption, to get at a more complete picture of any reported import penetration.

Even the apparently simple language of this first requirement, however, is not completely free of difficulty. Bale (1973, 135–37; 1974, 55) has pointed out a number of times in the literature that the interpretation of the term "directly competitive" is not at all clear-cut. Indeed, recognizing the difficulty, the Commission itself was divided on this very issue a number of times, mostly in cases involving footwear. Bale convincingly shows how, by defining shoes in general into narrow and specific TSUSA classes, it is always possible to find a class where imports have not increased, although imports of shoes in total may have increased significantly (Bale 1973, 136). As a possible way out, Bale suggested the application of the theoretical concept of the elasticity of substitution to a given set of imported and domestic goods to determine if they are directly competitive. The practical limitations of this procedure, however, are quickly recognized and acknowledged as not viable under present constraints (Bale 1973, 137).

2) The increased imports are in major part the result of trade concessions granted under trade agreements.

As a first step in determining whether there is a relationship between trade concessions and imports, the petitioner must show that the concessions were granted before the rise in imports took place. Two problems immediately surface. The first problem is to determine which are the relevant concessions. If a firm/worker claims injury due to increased imports in 1970–1974, for example, can this current injury be linked to a trade concession that was granted in 1934? Or should the relevant trade concession be one that was granted close in time to the current period of increased imports? The legislative history of the TEA seems to indicate that it views the aggregate of all concessions granted since 1934 and has consistently—although not always unanimously—considered the total reductions since the beginning of the trade agreements program, not necessarily only the most recent concessions granted.. Commissioners who have disagreed with the aggregation rule, have considered the effect of only the more recent concessions, while treating earlier reductions as "conditions of trade." They have asserted, in effect, that concessions granted years or even decades before imports increased have become part of the totality of market conditions and cannot be singled out as the major cause of increased imports. In a number of deliberations of women's footwear, for example, the fact that shoe imports were increasing before tariff concessions were granted was found to be sufficient evidence for the Commission to rule that the trade concessions had not induced the increased imports (TEA 1970). A further report on nonrubber footwear (TEA 1971) resulted in a divided finding, with some commissioners asserting that the time lag between the concessions and the increased imports was too long to have any relevance, and that even the Kennedy rounds reductions that began in 1968 were irrelevant because imports increased sharply prior to that date. Rather, attention was called to the disparity between United States and foreign wage rates, limited gains in American productivity, and rapid wage increases, all of which were held to be of greater importance than tariff reductions (TEA 1971).

A second, related problem, demands a show of causality between increased imports and trade concessions. Clearly, only a statistical test can provide an indication of such causality, The *Transmission Towers* (1969) and *Buttweld Pipe* (1968) cases indicate the difficulty in proving a cause and effect relationship between trade concessions and increased imports, and the extent to which the concessions were the most significant causal factor. The Commission, aware of the difficulty, made a clever change in procedure. Instead of attempting to prove that tariff reductions were in major part responsible for increased imports, the Commission substituted what has become known as the "but for" test. It concluded in the B*uttweld Pipe* that "we need ask ourselves only whether, but for the concessions, would import be substantially at their present level" (1968, 10).

The "but for" test may be interpreted in the following way: If, in the absence of trade concessions, imports would not have increased, then the "in major part" provision would be met. More formally, trade concessions may be the cause of increased imports if the occurrence of concessions is sufficient for the subsequent occurrence of increased imports. This would imply that whatever concessions are granted, increased imports follow in quick succession. The astounding implication is that a given concession must immediately induce a rise in imports, to be followed by immediate complaint from the industry. If there is a delayed reaction, the "major part" causal link between concessions and increased imports cannot be supported (Banner 1966, 1342). In addition, to test the stated hypothesis, all independent variables would have to be held constant, while trade concessions would represent the experimental variable.

To be sure, in the more recent period, the Commission has recognized that the chain of events indicated is not likely to be instantaneous (TEA 1964, 66). Normally, the physical plant in the exporting countries must be expanded to meet the increased demand cause for tariff reductions and a time lag between the two events should realistically be expected.

All in all, this second criterion has been appropriately called the "Achilles' heel" of the TEA (Bale 1974, 66). The Commission appears to have made the causal link between trade concessions and increased imports an impossible burden of proof.

3) The firm is seriously injured, or threatened with serious injury (or in the case of workers, a significant number or portion of the petitioning workers are unemployed or underemployed or are threatened with unemployment or underemployment).

On the whole, this requirement has not been difficult to meet. Out of 131 cases presented through 1971, only six have failed to substantiate serious injury (Bale 1974, 68). Whether the industry, firm, or workers are seriously injured is an undeniable fact demonstrated by the evidence presented at the hearings. In the footwear industry, for example, all recent evidence involving falling domestic production, frequency of plant closings, and imports at about one-third of domestic consumption, would seem to indicate that competitive injury has occurred and that it may well increase in the future. It is equally true, however, that the Commission has also insisted on examining the importance of factors other than imports before making its determination and, in a scattered number of cases, has found that imports were not the major factor causing or threatening serious injury.

4) The increased imports (resulting in major part from trade agreement concessions) have been the major factor causing or threatening to cause the serious injury (or, in the case of workers, the unemployment of underemployment).

The petitioner must now sustain the double burden of proving both that the increased imports were caused in major part by trade concessions and that the increased imports were the major factor in causing the serious injury. In this way, a preponderant dual causal link between trade concessions and increased imports and between increased imports and serious injury must be established. In so doing, the Commission appears to have made these tests an almost impossible burden of proof (Banner 1966, 1334).

As in the application of the second criterion, the Commission has not been successful in producing convincing evidence of cause-and-effect linkages between increased imports and injury, nor indeed, between any other condition of trade and injury. This should not be too surprising, since many of these injury-causing factors are not quantifiable and cannot be subjected to appropriate statistical calculations.

In summary, then, it would appear that determining the eligibility of an industry, firm, or group of workers for adjustment assistance under the foregoing criteria has been rather difficult, mostly because of the required double show of causality and because of the paucity of supporting data that could be fitted into a statistical model that could materially assist the decision process.

A number of proposals have been advanced in and out of the Congress to revise adjustment assistance. Some have been directed at overcoming problems related to the implementation of the program, while others urge a fundamentally different approach to the whole arrangement.

Reflecting the consensus of the times, President Richard Nixon, in his proposed Trade Act of 1969, called for a relaxation of the TEA criteria. The proposal required that the injury-causing increased imports should not be causally linked to prior trade agreement concessions. Further, such imports would not be required to be the major cause of serious injury, but only a substantial cause, with obviously different implications. Under the changes suggested in this proposal and in several variants of its (HR 18970, 1970), adjustment assistance could be provided to industries, firms, or workers regardless of the cause of increased imports.

Theoretical and Empirical Justification for TAA in the Post-NAFTA Era

While TAA was functioning before NAFTA, the Government intended its role to be strengthened during the post-NAFTA era. At the dawn of the NAFTA agreement, President Clinton anticipated the need for TAA by proposing a $100m in employment relief to aid NAFTA-displaced workers. (Aggarwal et al. 1998,142). According to Senator Orrin Hatch, at the dawn of NAFTA passage, Congress made a deal "with labor that they would acquiesce in open trade policies, and the government would provide training and income support for workers who lost their jobs as a result. That became the Trade Adjustment Assistance Program" (*Congressional Record*, 1993, S16413).

Traditional trade theory that requires labor and capital to be mobile within a country increasingly required TAA incentives as a prop for those goals. For instance, "the Dixit-Norman scheme of commodity taxes may not lead to strict Pareto gains from trade. Rather, this scheme must be augmented by policies that give factors an incentive to move between industries: hence, the role for trade adjustment assistance" (Feenstra 1994, 201). The conditions that Feenstra discusses to attain Pareto optimality pivots on two essential points. On the one hand, TAA must not be used simply as an income supplement, but as a means to transfer displaced workers from one industry or location to another. On the other hand, displaced workers should move to industries and locations where prices were increased because of international competition (Feenstra 2004, 186). In a similar vein, some writers extended Samuelson's 2 × 2 trade model to study trade impact on the US industries (Aggarwal et al. 1998, 139). Other writers adopted the Krugman differentiated product model to assess NAFTA (Kyoji et al. 2003, 7).

Models still evolve in consideration of the best way on how to use TAA. Carl Davidson and Steven Matusz (2004, 749) have advanced several scenarios for such assessments. In one case they used Samuelson intergenerational model. In that model,

> workers trade off the potentially higher wage that the export sector has to offer with a lower job acquisition rate. An unexpected improvement in the terms of trade surprises old workers who cannot undo the decisions they made while young. Some old workers who had not planned to search for work in the export sector end up changing their plans, adding to the pool of searchers, creating congestion. Temporary protection can reduce congestion and make the transition to the new steady state smoother.

They have also considered cases where workers may be trapped in a low-tech job due to trade impact, being unable to move, as well as cases where workers can move to other high-tech jobs through proper job searching (Davidson and Matusz June 2004). The situation at which Pareto optimality is achieved with TAA after import impact seem still indeterminate, and may require temporary wage or employment subsidies as an alternative to TAA in cases where workers have difficulty moving (Feenstra 2004, 186).

While tariff concessions may produce desirable results for the economy as a whole, they may produce adverse effects on a number of domestic industries particularly affected by changes in trade policy. When dislocations occur, the government must assume the responsibility to minimize the resulting market distortions and should absorb, at least in part, the cost of readjustment to alternate lines of activity. Adjustment assistance may be viewed as a prerequisite to foster the orderly transfer of resources by subsidizing those factors that are mostly impacted. Injury to firms and workers caused by import competition are corrected on a domestic rather than international level. That is, individual adjustment assistance is exclusively tailored to the needs of firms that are in difficulty and workers who have lost their jobs. Helping them would, of course, entail some cost to the taxpayer on the justification that these firms and workers are the victims of a national policy of trade liberalization. The benefits of that policy to consumers (taxpayers) and to the economy would normally be greater than the costs incurred for adjustment assistance, as our estimates of costs and benefits have shown.

Economists see economic openness as leading in general to higher living standards, even though it can also cause significant losses of jobs and idling of capital capacity. Furthermore, the quantitative estimates of consumer gains from globalization do not include such intangibles as a greater range of choice open to consumers afforded by greater variety, styles, and comfort available in the import mix or the erosion of existing class and racial barriers. Neither do the estimates of losses resulting from unemployment include the possible psychological and social costs to the affected individuals, such as the impact of unemployment on physical and mental illness, mortality rates, and deterioration of family relations. There is much to be said about the need of government intervention to expand existing trade adjustment assistance programs, which provide resources to individuals displaced by import impacted changes and make lives more stable and secure.

It may be argued—on equity considerations—that there is no valid reason why workers and firms displaced by import competition should receive special compensation that those displaced for other economic reasons do not receive. The failure of conventional macro policy to sustain full employment and to ease the reabsorption of displaced resources had dramatically brought home the fact that import impact is only one of many possible causes of economic dislocation and unemployment. To compensate injury due to import competition without commensurate compensation for other government-induced injury is discriminatory and inequitable.

Adjustment assistance does not imply that there is something basically wrong with market forces. It is, rather, an acceptance of the reality of international competition which, at times, prevents free market directives from operating efficiently everywhere. Import impact, for example, coincided with the rapid increases in imports since NAFTA. Admittedly, American wage rates have been higher than in the rest of the world but, historically, they have been offset by the higher productivity of American labor, as enhanced by the recent high-tech revolution from the inception of NAFTA. However, the mobility of capital on the global scale, and the lag in the development of international laws governing property rights has weakened the United States in the world markets especially in the areas of manufacturing.

It is clear, then, that the logic of trade adjustment assistance rests in part on the realities of changing patterns of competition in international trade and the related obligation of government to ease the resulting economic dislocations. The process of adjustment may not work perfectly, since it is often difficult to determine precisely the relationship between import penetration and the scores of other factors causing dislocation. However, the concepts of retraining, job search, and relocation, which are part of the whole package of adjustment assistance, are basically good and could be made viable given favorable conditions. The resulting benefits of both the workers and society of a real adjustment program could be very substantial. The workers could quickly regain productive employment, probably in a better position, with renewed income and pride. Society would also gain by removing the unemployed workers from the public rolls and add them to the producing side of the ledger, thus benefiting from both decreased transfer payments and increased production and tax revenues.

How the enhancement to TAA in the post NAFTA era has affected the distressed industries is the story of this book. By encouraging the imports of consumer products, and the mobility of US capital and companies to Canada and Mexico, NAFTA has increased competition for the distressed industries. The

North American Integration and Development (NAID) Center at UCLA has been keeping score of job displacements, sourcing the job losses to areas in the country that are most impacted, the industries that are affected, and the amount of TAA benefits received. All in all, as the estimates we provide, TAA benefits prop up the industries impacted. The need for TAA has not been undermined. Just the opposite. As for the United States' trade deficit with Mexico and Canada it has increased steadily: $112.2 billion, $115.9B, $129.2 b, $154.4 billion for the years 2001, 2002, 2003, and 2004 respectively. TAA can be thus seen as a way to help the enhancement of the impacted industries in the face of this new competitive challenge.

Bibliography

Abdelkhalek, Touhami and Jean-Marie Dufour, "Statistical Inference for Computable General Equilibrium Models, with Application to a Model of the Moroccan Economy," *Review of Economics and Statistics*, Vol. 80, November, 1998, pp. 520–34.

Abernathy, Frederick, H., John T. Dunlop, Janice H. Hammond, and David Weil, "The Information-Integrated Channel: A Study of the US Apparel Industry in Transition," *Brookings Papers on Economic Activities: Microeconomics*, 1995, pp. 175–246.

Adams, Walter and Joel B. Dirlam, "Steel Imports and Vertical Oligopoly Power," *American Economic Review*, Vol. 54, Issue 5, September, 1964, pp. 626–35.

Adams, Walter and Joel B. Dirlam, "Steel Imports and Vertical Oligopoly Power: Reply," *American Economic Review*, Vol. 56, Issue 1/2, March, 1966, pp. 160–68.

Adams, Walter and Joel B. Dirlam, "Steel Imports and Vertical Oligopoly Power: Reply," *American Economic Review*, Vol. 57, Issue 4, September, 1967, pp. 917–19.

Adams, Walter, "The Steel Industry," in Walter Adams, ed., *The Structure of American Industry*, 5th edn (New York: Macmillan, 1977), pp. 86–129.

Adams, Walter, "Steel," in Walter Adams and James W. Brock, eds, *The Structure of American Industry*, 9th edn (Englewood Cliffs, NJ: Prentice Hall, 1995), pp. 93–118.

Adams, Walter and James W. Brock, *The Bigness Complex*, 2nd edn (Stanford University Press, 2004).

Aggarwal, Raj, Michael Long, Scott Moore and Danny Ervin, "Industry Differences in NAFTA's Impact on the Valuation of US Companies," *International Review of Financial Analysis*, Vol. 7, No. 2, 1998, 137–52.

Aggarwal, Vinod, K., and Stephan Haggard, "The Politics of Protection in the US Textile and Apparel Industries," in John Zysman and Laura Tyson, eds, *American Industry in International Competition* (New York: Cornell University Press, 1983), pp. 249–312.

Agrawal, M., *Global Competitiveness in the Pharmaceutical Industry* (Binghamton, NY: The Haworth Press, 1999).

Aho, C. Michael and Thomas O. Bayard. "Costs and Benefits of Trade Adjustment Assistance," in Robert E. Baldwin and Anne O. Krueger, eds, *The Structure and Evolution of Recent US Trade Policy* (Chicago, IL: University of Chicago Press, 1984).

Aliprantis, C.D., D.J. Brown, and O. Burkinshaw, *Existence and Optimality of Competitive Equilibria* (New York: Springer-Verlag, 1990).

Armington, Paul S., "The Geographic Pattern of Trade and The Effects of Price Changes," *International Monetary Fund Staff Papers*, 1969, pp. 179–99.

Armington, Paul S., "A Theory of Demand for Products Distinguished by Place of Production," *International Monetary Fund Staff Papers*, 1969, pp. 159–76.

Association of American Publishers, Inc. (AAP) "Contractual Licensing, Technological Measures and Copyright Law" (www. Publishers.org/confpub/index.htm), 2002, pp. 1–13.

Averyt, William F. and K. Ramagopal, "Strategic Disruption and Transaction Cost Economics: The Case of the American Auto Industry and Japanese Competition," *International Business Review*, Vol. 8, 1999, pp. 39–53.

Bagwell, Kyle and Robert W. Staiger. "A Theory of Managed Trade," *American Economic Review*, Vol. 80, No. 4, September, 1990, pp. 779–95.

Bagwell, Kyle and Robert W. Staiger, *The Economics of The World Trading System* (Cambridge, MA: The MIT Press, 2002).

Bain, Joe S., *Industrial Organization* (New York: John Wiley and Sons, Inc., 1959).

Bain, Joe S., *Barriers to New Competition* (Cambridge, MA: Harvard University Press, 1956).

Balance, R., J. Pogany, and H. Forstner, *The World's Pharmaceutical Industries: An International Perspective on Innovation, Competition, and Policy* (Aldershot, UK: Edward Elgar, 1992).

Balassa, Bela, *Trade Liberalization among Industrial Countries: Objectives and Alternatives* (New York: McGraw-Hill Book Company, 1967).

Balassa, Bela, "A Changing Pattern of Comparative Advantage in Manufactured Goods," *Review of Economics and Statistics*, 61(2), May, 1979, pp. 259–66.

Baldwin, Robert E., "Equilibrium in International Trade: A Diagrammatic Analysis," *Quarterly Journal of Economics*, Vol. 63, No. 5, November, 1948, pp. 748–62.

Baldwin, Robert E., "Determinants of the Commodity Structure of US Trade," *American Economic Review*, Vol. 61, No. 1, March, 1971, pp. 126–46.

Baldwin, Robert E., "Determinants of the Commodity Structure of US Trade: Reply," *American Economic Review*, Vol. 62, No. 3, June, 1972, p. 465.

Bale, M.D., "Adjustment to Freer Trade: An Analysis of the Adjustment Assistance Provision of the Trade Expansion Act of 1962," prepared for the Manpower Administration, US Department of Labor (Washington, DC).

Bale, M.D., "Comment," *Southern Economic Journal*, Vol. 40, No. 2, October 1973, pp. 135–8.

Bale, M.D., "Adjustment Assistance under the Trade Expansion Act of 1962," *Journal of International Law and Economics*, Vol. 9, April, 1974, p. 49.

Banerjee, Anindya, Juan Dolado, John W. Galbraith, and David F. Henry, *Co-Integration, Error-Correction, and the Econometric Analysis of Non-Stationary Data* (Oxford: Oxford University Press, 1993).

Banner, T.K., "In Major Part"—The New Causation Problem in the Trade Agreements Program," *Texas Law Review*, Vol. 44 (1965–66), p. 1331.

Bergson, Abram, *Welfare, Planning, and Employment: Selected Essays in Economic Theory* (Cambridge, MA: The MIT Press, 1982).

Berndt, E.R., I.M. Cockburn, and Z. Griliches, "Pharmaceutical Innovations and Market Dynamics: Tracking Effects on Price Indexes for Antidepressant Drugs," *Brookings Papers on Economic Activity*, 1997, pp. 133–99.

Berndt, E.R., R.S. Pindyck and P. Azoulay, "Consumption Externalities and Diffusion in Pharmaceutical Markets: Antiulcer Drugs," *NBER Working Paper* 7772, June 2000.

Berry, Steven, James Levinsohn, and Ariel Pakes, "Voluntary Export Restraints on Automobiles: Evaluating a Trade Policy," *American Economic Review*, Vol. 89, No. 3, June, 1999, pp. 400–30.

Bhagwati, Jagdish N., ed., *Essays in International Economic Theory*, vols 1 and 2 (Cambridge, MA: The MIT Press, 1983).

Bhagwati, Jagdish N., *Protectionism* (Cambridge, MA: The MIT Press, 1988).

Bhagwati, Jagdish N., Arvind Panagariya and T.N. Srinivasan, *Lectures on International Trade*, 2nd edn (Cambridge, MA: The MIT Press, 1998).

Bhagwati, Jagdish N., *Free Trade Today* (Princeton, NJ: Princeton University Press, 2002).

Bishop, William R., "Investigations Completed Under Section 201 of the Trade Act of 1974," unpublished, USITC, Washington, DC (2002) cited in Davidson and Matusz, 2004, 749.

Bittlingmayer, G, "Resale Price Maintenance in the Book Trade with an Application to Germany, " *Journal of Institutional and Theoretical Economics*, Vol. 44, No. 1, 1988, pp. 789–812.

Bittlingmayer, G, "The Elasticity of Demand for Books, Resale Price Maintenance and the Lerner Index," *Journal of Institutional and Theoretical Economics*, Vol. 148, No. 4, 1992, pp. 588–606.

Blair, J. le, "Price Discrimination in Steel: A Reply," *American Economic Review* Vol. 33 No. 22, June, 1943, pp. 369–70.

Book Industry Group, Inc., *Book Industry Trends*, 2000.

Brander, James A., "Strategic Trade Policy," NBER Working Paper No. 5020, February, 1995. Also in G. Grossman and K. Rogoff, *Handbook of International Economics*, vol. III (Amsterdam: Elsevier, 1995), pp. 1397–444.

Brander, James A. and Barbara J. Spencer, "Tariffs and the Extraction of Foreign Monopoly Rents under Potential Entry," *The Canadian Journal of Economics*, Vol. 14, No. 3, August, 1981, pp. 371–89.

Bratt, H.A., "Assisting the Economic Recovery of Import-Injured Firms," *Law and Policy in International Business*, Vol. 6 (1974).

Brynjolfsson, Erick and Lorin M. Hitt, "Beyond Computation: Information Technology, Organization Transformation and Business Performance," *Journal of Economic Perspectives*, Vol. 14, No. 4, Fall, 2000, pp. 23–48.

Brynjolfsson, Erick, "High-Technology Industries and Market Structure: Comment," in *Economic Policy for the Information Economy* (Kansas City: The Federal Reserve Bank of Kansas City, 2001), pp. 103–10.

Bultuck, R. and R. Litan, *Down in the Dumps* (Washington, DC: Brookings Institution, 1991).

Buttweld Pipe, TEA-W-8 (1968).

Caves, R.E., M.D. Whinston, and M.A. Hurwitz, "Patent Expiration, Entry, and Competition in the US Pharmaceutical Industry," *Brookings Papers on Economic Activity*, 1991, pp. 1–45.

Chichilnisky, Graciela and Geoffrey Heal, *The Evolving International Economy* (New York: Cambridge University Press, 1986).

Chichilnisky, Graciela, "Traditional Comparative Advantages vs. Economics of Scale: NAFTA and GATT," in Mario Baldassarri, Massimo Di Matteo, and Robert Mundell, *International Problems of Economic Interdependence* (London: St Martin's Press, 1994), pp. 161–97.

Choi, J.P., "Herd Behavior, The 'Penguin Effect,' and the Suppression of Informational Diffusion: An Analysis of Informational Externalities and Payoff Interdependency," *RAND Journal of Economics*, Vol. 28, No. 3, Autumn, 1997, pp. 403–25.

Chung, Jae W., "Effects of US Trade Remedy Law Enforcement under Uncertainty: The Case of Steel," *Southern Economic Journal*, 1998, Vol. 65, No. 1, pp. 151–9.

Cline, W. R., *The Future of World Trade in Textile and Apparel* (Washington, DC: Institute for International Economics, 1987).

Cline, William, *Trade Policy and Global Poverty* (Washington, DC: Institute for International Economics, 2004).

Co, Cathrine Y., "Japanese FDI into the US Automobile Industry: An Empirical Investigation," *Japan and the World Economy*, Vol. 9, 1997, pp. 93–108.

Comanor, W.S., "The Political Economy of the Pharmaceutical Industry," *Journal of Economic Literature*, Vol. 24, Issue 3, September, 1986, pp. 1178–217.

Commons, John R., "The Delivered Price Practice in the Steel Market," *American Economic Review*, Vol. 14, Issue 3 (September, 1924), pp. 505–19.

Corden, W.M., *Trade Policy and Economic Welfare* (Oxford: Oxford University Press, 1974).

Craft, N.F.R. and Mark Thomas, "Comparative Advantage in UK Manufacturing Trade, 1910–1935," *The Economic Journal*, Vol. 96, No. 282, September, 1986, pp. 629–45.

Crandall, Robert W., "The Effect of US Trade Protection for Autos and Steel," *Brookings Papers on Economic Activity,* No. 1, 1987, pp. 271–88.

Curwen, Peter J., "The Economics of Academic Publishing in the UK," *Journal of Industrial Economics*, March, 1977, pp. 161–75.

Danzon, P.M., *Pharmaceutical Price Regulation* (Washington, DC: The AEI Press, 1997).

Davidson, Carl and Steven J. Matusz, "Trade Liberalization and Compensation," (February 2002, Revised June 2004), unpublished paper available at http://www.msu.edu/%7Edavidso4/TradeLiberalizationandCompensationRevised.pdf.

Davidson, Carl and Steven J. Matusz, "An Overlapping-generations Model of Escape Clause Protection," *Review of International Economics*, Vol.12, No. 5 (November, 2004), pp. 749–68.

De Vany, Arthur and Gail Frey, "Backlogs and the Value of Excess Capacity in the Steel Industry," *American Economic Review*, Vol. 72, Issue 3, June, 1982, pp. 441–51.

Deardorff, Alan V. and Robert M. Stern, "The Structure of Tariff Protection: Effects of Foreign Tariffs and Existing NTBs," *Review of Economics and Statistics*, Vol. 67, No. 4, November, 1985, pp. 539–48.

Dixit, Avinash K., "Optimal Trade and Industrial Policies for the US Automobile Industry," in Robert C. Freenstra, ed., *Empirical Methods for International Trade* (Cambridge, MA: The MIT Press, 1989), pp. 141–70.

Dixit, Avinash K. and Victor Norman, *Theory of International Trade* (London: James Nisbet-Welwyn, 1980).

Dixit, Avinash K. and Victor Norman, "Gains from Trade Without Lump-Sum Compensation," *Journal of International Economics*, Vol. 21, 1986, pp. 111–22.

Dornbusch, Rudiger, *Stabilization, Debt, and Reform* (Englewood Cliffs, NJ: Prentice Hall, 1993).

Dornbusch, Rudiger and Sebastian Edwards, *Reform, Recovery and Growth* (Chicago, IL: University of Chicago Press, 1995).

Dunning, J.H., "International Direct Investment in Innovation: The Pharmaceutical Industry," in *Multinationals, Technology, and Competitiveness* (London: Unwin Hyman, 1988).

Edgeworth, F.Y., "Theory of International Values," *The Economic Journal*, Vol. 4, No. 13, March, 1894, pp. 35–50; Vol. 4, No. 15, September, 1894, Vol. 4, No. 16, December, 1894, pp. 606–38.

Edgeworth, F.Y. "Disputed Points in the Theory of International Trade," *The Economic Journal*, Vol. 11, No. 44, December, 1901, pp. 582–95.

Ellison, S.F., I. Cockburn, Z. Griliches, and J. Hausman, "Characteristics of Demand for Pharmaceutical Products: An Examination of Four Cephalosporins," *RAND Journal of Economics*, Vol. 28, No. 3, Autumn, 1997, pp. 426–46.

Engle, R.F. and C.W.J. Granger, *Long-Run Economic Relationships: Readings in Cointegration* (Oxford: Oxford University Press, 1991).

Engle, Robert F., *ARCH: Selected Readings* (Oxford: Oxford University Press, 1995).

Federal Reserve Bank of Kansas City (FRB), *Economic Policy for the Information Economy* (Kansas City: The Federal Reserve Bank of Kansas City, 2001).

Feenstra, Robert, C., ed., *Empirical Methods for International Trade* (Cambridge, MA: The MIT Press, 1989).

Feenstra, Robert C., "Gains from Trade in Differentiated Products: Japanese Compact Trucks," in Robert C. Feenstra, ed., *Empirical Methods for International Trade* (Cambridge, MA: The MIT Press, 1989).

Feenstra, Robert C. and Tracy R. Lewis, "Trade Adjustment Assistance and Pareto Gains from Trade," *Journal of International Economics*, Vol. 36, Issues 3–4 (May 1994), pp. 201–22.

Feenstra, Robert C., *Advanced International Trade: Theory and Evidence* (Princeton, NJ: Princeton University Press, 2004).

Findlay, Ronald, *Factor Proportions, Trade, and Growth* (Cambridge, MA: The MIT Press, 1995).

Fooks, M.M., "Trade Adjustment Assistance," in the *United States International Policy in an Interdependent World*, report to the President submitted by the Commission on Int. Trade and Investment Policy, Compendium I (July, 1972).

Frank, R.G. and D. Salkever, "Pricing, Patent Loss and the Market for Pharmaceuticals," *Southern Economic Journal*, Vol. 59, No. 2, October, 1992, pp. 165–79.

Freeman, Richard B. and Morris M. Kleiner. "The Last American Shoe Manufacturers: Changing the Method of Pay to Survive Foreign Competition," NBER Working Paper 6750, October 1998.

Fudenberg, D. and J. Tirole, *Game Theory* (Cambridge, MA: The MIT Press, 1993).

Gale Research, *Encyclopedia of Global Industry*, 1996.

Fung, K.C. and R.W. Staiger, "Trade Liberalization and Trade Adjustment Assistance," in M. Canzoneri, W. Ethier, and V. Grilli, eds., *The New Transatlantic Economy* (Cambridge: Cambridge University Press, 1996).

Ghadar, Fariborz, William H. Davidson, and Charles S. Feigenoff, *US Industrial Competitiveness: The Case of the Textile and Apparel Industries* (Lexington, MA: Lexington Books, 1987).

Ghemawat, Pankaj, *Games Businesses Play: Cases and Models* (Cambridge, MA: The MIT Press, 1997).

Gordon, Robert J., "Does the 'New Economy' Measure up to the Great Inventions of the Past?," *Journal of Economic Perspectives*, Vol. 14, No. 4, Fall, 2000, pp. 49–74.

Grabowski, H., "The Determinants of R&D in Three Industries," *Journal of Political Economy*, Vol. 76, 1968.

Grabowski, H. and Mueller, D.C., "Non-Price Competition in the Cigarette Industry," *The Antitrust Bulletin*, Vol. 14, 1969, pp. 607–28.

Grabowski, H. and Mueller, D.C., "Non-Price Competition in the Cigarette Industry: A Comment," *The Antitrust Bulletin*, Vol. 14, 1970, pp. 679–86.

Grabowski, H.G. and Mueller, D.C., "Imitative Advertising in the Cigarette Industry," *The Antitrust Bulletin*, Vol. 16, Summer, 1971, pp. 257–92.

Grabowski, H.G. and N.D. Baxter, "Rivalry in Industrial Research and Development," *Journal of Industrial Economics*, Vol. 21, No. 3, 1973. pp. 209–35.

Grabowski, H.G. and J.M. Vernon, "Innovation and Invention: Consumer Protection Regulation in Ethical Drugs," *American Economic Review Proceedings*, Vol. 67, No. 1, 1977, pp. 359–64.

Grabowski, H.G. and J.M. Vernon, "A New Look at the Returns and Risks of Pharmaceutical R&D," *Management Science*, Vol. 36, July 1990, pp. 804–21.

Grandmont, J. M. and D. McFadden, "A Technical Note on Classical Gains from Trade," *Journal of International Economics*, Vol. 2, 1972, pp. 109–25.

Granger, Clive W.J., *Empirical Modeling in Economics: Specification and Evaluation* (New York: Cambridge University Press, 1999).

Griliches, Z., "Patent Statistics as Economic Indicators: A Survey," *Journal of Economic Literature*, Vol. 28, December, 1990, pp. 1661–707.

Haberler, Gottfried, "Some Problems in the Pure Theory of International Trade," *Economic Journal,* Vol. 60, June, 1950, pp. 223–40.

Hahn, F.H., "On General Equilibrium and Stability," in E. Cary Brown and Robert M. Solow, eds, *Paul Samuelson and Modern Economic Theory* (New York : Mc Graw-Hill Book Company, 1983).

Hall, Christopher G.L., *Steel Phoenix: The Fall and Rise of the US Steel Industry* (New York: St Martin's Press, 1997).

Harcourt, G.C., "The Cambridge Controversies: Old Ways and New Horizons-Or Dead End?," *Oxford Economic Papers*, New Series, Vol. 28, No. 1, March, 1976, pp. 25–65.

Harrison. Glenn W., Thomas F. Rutherford, and David G. Tarr, "Quantifying the Uruguay Round," *The Economic Journal*, Vol. 107, September, 1997, pp. 1405–30.

Hay, D.A. and D.J. Morris, *Industrial Economics: Theory and Evidence* (New York: Oxford University Press, 1979).

Hayek, F.A., *The Collected Works of F. A. Hayek*, vol. 1: *The Fatal Conceit*, W.W. Bartley III, ed. (Chicago, IL: University of Chicago Press, 1988).

Hekman, John S., "An Analysis of the Changing Location of Iron and Steel Production in the Twentieth Century," *American Economic Review*, Vol. 68, Issue 1, March, 1978, pp. 123–33.

Herbener, Jeffrey M., "The Pareto Rule and Welfare Economics," *Review of Austrian Economics*, Vol. 10, No. 1, 1997.

Hertel, Thomas W. and Marinos E. Tsigas, "The Structure of GTAP," in Thomas W. Hertel, ed., *Global Trade Analysis* (London: Cambridge University Press, 1998).

Hicks, John R., *Essays in World Economics* (Oxford: Clarendon Press, 1959), cited in Jagdish Bhagwati, *Free Trade Today* (Princeton, NJ: Princeton University Press, 2002).

Hoover, Kevin D., *Causality in Macroeconomics* (New York: Cambridge University Press, 2001).

H.R. 18970, 91st Congress, 2nd Session, 1970, the "Trade-Bill"; H.R. 16920, and "Mills Bill."

Hufbauer, Gary Clyde and Howard F. Rosen, *Trade Policy for Distressed Industries* (Washington, DC: Institute for International Economics, March, 1986).

Hufbauer, Gary C. and Jeffrey J. Schott. *North American Free Trade: Issues and Recommendations* (Washington, DC: Institute for International Economics, 1992).

Hufbauer, Gary C. and Kimberley A. Elliot, *Measuring the Costs of Protection for the United States* (Washington, DC: Institute for International Economics, 1994).

Hufbauer, Gary C., Kimberley A. Elliot, Tess Cyrus, and Elizabeth Winston, *US Economic Sanctions: Their Impact on Trade, Jobs, and Wages* (Washington, DC: Institute for International Economics, Working Paper: 1997).

Ikenson, Dan, *Steel Trap: How Subsidies and Protectionism Weaken the US Industry* (Trade Briefing Papers from the Cato Institute, No. 14, March, 2002).

International Trade Administration (ITA), United States Department of Commerce, Office of Automotive Affairs, "Compilation of Foreign Motor Vehicle Import Requirements," December, 2003.

Irwin, Douglas, "Changes in US Tariffs: The Role of Import Prices and Commercial Policies," *American Economic Review*, Vol. 88, No. 4, September, 1998, pp. 1015–26.

Irwin, Douglas, "Did Late-Nineteenth-Century US Tariffs Promote Infant Industries? Evidence from the Tinplate Industry," *The Journal of Economic History*, Vol. 60, No. 2, 2000, pp. 335–60.

Jaffe, E.D. and H, L, Nagel, "Import Competition and Adjustment Assistance," paper presented to the *Eastern Economic Association Meeting*, Albany, NY (October, 1974).

Judge, George G., R. Carter Hill, William E. Griffiths, Helmut Lutkepohl, and Tsoung-Chao Lee, *Introduction to the Theory and Practice of Econometrics* (New York: John Wiley & Sons, 1988).

Kamien, M.I. and N.L. Schwartz, "Market Structure, Elasticity of Demand, and the Incentive to Invest," *Journal of Law and Economics*, Vol. 13, No. 1, 1970, p. 241.

Kamien, M.I. and N.L. Schwartz, "Market Structure and Innovation: A Survey," *Journal of Economic Literature*, Vol. 13, Issue 1, March, 1975, pp. 1–37.

Kapstein, Ethan B., "Winners and Losers in the Global Economy," *International Organization*, Vol. 54, No. 2, Spring, 2000, pp. 359–84.

Kaufman, Bruce E., "An Interview with Steelworkers' President Lynn Williams," *Journal of Labor Research*, Winter, 2001, pp. 145–51.

Kemp, Murray C., "The Gain from International Trade," *The Economic Journal*, Vol. 72, No. 288, December, 1962, pp. 803–19.

Kemp, Murray C. and Henry Y. Wan, Jr, " *International Economic Review*, Vol. 13, No. 3, October, 1972, pp. 509–22.

Kenen, Peter B., *The International Economy*, 3rd edn (New York: Cambridge University Press, 1994).

Keynes, John Maynard, *Essays in Persuasion* (New York: W.W. Norton & Company, Inc., 1963).

Kolassa, E.M., *Elements of Pharmaceutical Pricing* (Binghamton, NY: The Haworth Press, 1997).

Krauss, Melvyn B. and Harry G. Johnson, *General Equilibrium Analysis* (London: George Allen & Unwin, 1974).

Kreps, David M., *A Course in Microeconomic Theory* (Princeton, NJ: Princeton University Press, 1990).

Krueger, Anne O., "Globalization: Preserving the Benefits," *OECD Observer*, December, 2003.

Krueger, Anne O. and Baran Tuncer. "An Empirical Test of the Infant Industry Argument," *American Economic Review*, Vol. 72, No. 5, December, 1982, pp. 1142–52.

Krugman, Paul, *Peddling Prosperity* (New York: W.W Norton & Company, 1994a).

Krugman, Paul, *Rethinking International Trade* (Cambridge, MA: The MIT Press, 1994b).

Kuh, Edwin and Richard L. Schmalensee, *An Introduction to Applied Macroeconomics* (Amsterdam: Elsevier Publishing Company, 1973).

Kyoji Fukao, Kyoji, Toshihiro Okubo, and Robert M. Stern, "An Econometric Analysis of Trade Diversion under NAFTA," *North American Journal of Economics and Finance*, Vol. 14, 2003, pp. 3–24.

Lee, Eric Youngkoo, and Michael Szenberg. "The Price, Quantity and Welfare Effects of US Trade Protection: The Case of Footwear," *International Economic Journal*, Vol. 2, No. 4, Winter, 1988, pp. 95–110.

Lee, Eric Youngkoo and Michael Szenberg "Analysis of Factors Determining Book Consumption in the United States, 1952–1985," in Douglas V. Shaw, William S. Hendon, and Virginia Lee Owen, eds, *Cultural Economics, An American Perspective* (Akron, OH: Association for Cultural Economics, 1990).

Lenway, Stefanie, Randall Morck and Bernard Yeung, "Rent Seeking, Protectionism and Innovation in the American Steel Industry," *The Economic Journal*, Vol. 106, March, 1996, pp. 410–21.

Leontief, Wassily W., *The Structure of American Economy* (New York: Oxford University Press, 1953).

Levitt, B. and J.G. March, "Chester I. Barnard and the Intelligence of Learning," in Oliver E. Williamson, ed., *Organization Theory* (New York: Oxford University Press, 1990), pp. 11–37.

Levy, R., *The Pharmaceutical Industry: A Discussion of Competitive and Antitrust Issues in an Environment of Change* (Washington, DC: Bureau of Economics Staff Report, Federal Trade Commission, March, 1999).

List, Friedrich, *The International System of Political Economy*, 1841, translated by Sampson S. Lloyd. Reprint (London: Longman, Green, 1885).

Machlup, Fritz, "Publishing Scholarly Books and Journals: Is it Economically Viable?," *Journal of Political Economy*, 85(1), February, 1977, pp. 217–25.

Magee, S.P., "How Much of Current Unemployment Did We Import" and "The Welfare Effects of Restrictions on US Trade," in *Brookings Papers on Economic Activity*, Nos 2 and 3 (1972).

Mankiw, N. Gregory, *Principles of Microeconomics*, 3rd edn (Mason: Thompson South-Western, 2004).

Mansfield, E., *The Economics of Technology Change* (New York: Norton, 1968).

Mansfield, E., "Basic Research and Productivity Increases in Manufacturing," *American Economic Review*, Vol. 70, Issue 5, December, 1980, pp. 863–73.

Mansfield, E., "Technological Change and Market Structure: An Empirical Study," *American Economic Review*, Vol. 73, Issue 2, May, 1983, pp. 205–9.

Mansfield, E., "Patents and Innovation: An Empirical Study," *Management Science*, Vol. 32, No. 2, February, 1986, pp. 173–81.

Mansfield, E., "Industrial R&D in Japan and the United States: A Comparative Study," *American Economic Review*, Vol. 78, Issue 2, May, 1988, pp. 223–8.

Marengo, Louis, "The Basing Point Decisions and the Steel Industry," *American Economic Review*, Vol. 45, Issue 2, Papers and Proceedings of the 67th Annual Meeting of the American Economic Association, May, 1955, pp. 509–22.

Matsuyama, Kiminori, "Perfect Equilibria in a Trade Liberalization Game," *American Economic Review*, Vol. 80, No. 3, June, 1990, pp. 480–92.

McFadyen, Jacquline, "NAFTA Supplemental Agreements: Four Year Review," Institute for International Economics Working Paper, 1998.

Meade, James, Edward, *A Geometry of International Trade* (London: Allen & Unwin, Ltd., 1956).

Measday, W., "The Pharmaceutical Industry," in Walter Adams, ed., *The Structure of American Industry*, 5th edn (New York: Macmillan, 1977), pp. 250–84.

Melo, Jaime de and David Tarr, "The Costs of US Quotas in Textile, Steel and Autos," *Review of Economics and Statistics*, Vol. 72, No. 3, August, 1990.

Mill, John Stuart, *Essays on Economics and Society, Collected Works of John Stuart Mill*, vol. IV, edited by J.M. Robson, with an Introduction by Lord Robbins (Toronto: University of Toronto Press, 1967).

Mittelhauser, Mark, "Employment Trends in Textiles and Apparel," 1973–2005, *Monthly Labor Review*, August, 1997, pp. 24–35.

Morck, Randall, Jungsywan Sepanski, and Bernard Yeung, "Habitual and Occasional Lobbyers in the US Steel Industry: An EM Algorithm," *Economic Inquiry*, Vol. 39, Issue 3, July 2001, pp. 365–78.

Mundell, Robert, "International Trade and Factor Mobility," *American Economic Review*, Vol. 47, 1957, pp. 321–35.

NAE, *The Competitive Status of the US Pharmaceutical Industry: The Influences of Technology in Determining Industrial Competitive Advantage* (Washington, DC: National Academy Press, 1983).

Nordhaus, William D., "Productivity Growth and the New Economy," *Brookings Papers on Economic Activities*, Vol. 2, 2002, pp. 211–44.

Pakes, A., "Comments and Discussion on Richard E. Caves, Michael D. Whinston, and Mark A. Hurwitz, 'Patent Expiration, Entry, and Competition in the US Pharmaceutical Industry,'" *Brookings Papers on Economic Activity*, 1991, pp. 1–45.

Pareto, Vilfredo, *Manual of Political Economy*, 1971 translation of 1927 edition (New York: Augustus M. Kelley, 1906).

Pareto, Vilfredo, "The New Theories of Economics," *Journal of Political Economy*, Vol. 5, No. 4, June, 1897, pp. 485–502.

Phillips, A., "Concentration, Scale and Technological Change in Selected Manufacturing Industries, 1899–1939," *Journal of Industrial Economics*, June, 1956.

Pindyck, Robert S. and Daniel L. Rubinfeld, *Econometric Models and Economic Forecasts*, 4th edn (New York: McGraw-Hill Irwin, 1998).

Ramrattan, Lall, Frank diMeglio, and Michael Szenberg, "The Effect of Telecom Density Data on Growth, Efficiencies, and Distributions in Global Economies," *Journal of Financial Transformation*, Capco Institute, Vol. 11, 2004.

Reinganum, J., "Practical Implications of Game Theoretic Models of R&D," *American Economic Review*, Vol. 74, Issue 2, May, 1984, pp. 61–6.

Ricardo, David. *The Principles of Political Economy and Taxation* (London: Dent & Sons, 1926).

Richardson, J. David, "Trade Adjustment Assistance Under the United States Trade Act of 1974: An Analytical Examination and Worker Survey," in Jagdish N. Bhagwati, *Import Competition and Response* (Chicago, IL: University of Chicago Press, 1982).

Robinson, Joan, *Essays in the Theory of Economic Growth* (London: Macmillan Press, 1962).

Romer, Paul M., "Exogenous Technical Change," *Journal of Political Economy*, Vol. 98, No. 5, Part 2, October, 1990, pp. S71–S102.

Romer, Paul M., "Implementing a National Technology Strategy with Self-Organizing Industry Investment Boards," *Brookings Papers on Economics Activity, Microeconomics* No. 1993.

Rosen, Ellen Israel, *The Globalization of the US Apparel Industry: Making Sweatshops* (Berkeley, CA: University of California Press, 2002).

Samuelson, Paul A. "An Extension of the Le Chatelier Principle," *Econometrica*, Vol. 28, 2, April, 1960, pp. 368–79.

Samuelson, Paul A., *The Collected Scientific Papers of Paul A. Samuelson*, vol. 2 (Cambridge, MA: The MIT Press, 1966).

Samuelson, Paul A., *The Collected Scientific Papers of Paul A. Samuelson*, vol. 5 (Cambridge, MA: The MIT Press, 1986).

Scherer, F.M., "Research and Development Resource Allocation Under Rivalry," *Quarterly Journal of Economics*, Vol. 81, No. 3, August, 1967, pp. 359–94.

Scherer, F. M., *Industrial Market Structure and Economic Performance*, 2nd edn (Chicago, IL: Rand McNally, 1980).

Scherer, F.M. and David Ross, *Industrial Market Structure and Economic Performance*, 3rd edn (Boston: Houghton Mifflin Company, 1990).

Scherer, F.M., "Pricing, Profits, and Technological Progress in the Pharmaceutical Industry," *Journal of Economic Perspectives*, Vol. 7, No. 3, Summer, 1993, pp. 97–115.

Scherer, F.M., *New Perspectives on Economic Growth and Technological Innovation* (Washington, DC: Brookings Institution Press, 1999).

Schlie, Erik and George Yip, "Regional Follows Global: Strategy Mixes in the World's Automotive Industry," *European Management Journal*, Vol. 18, No. 4, August, 2000.

Schumpeter, Joseph, *Business Cycles, A Theoretical, Historical, and Statistical Analysis of Capitalist Process*, vol. 1 (New York: McGraw-Hill Book Company, 1939).

Schwartzman, David, "Production and Productivity in the Service Industries," in Victor R.Fuchs, ed., *Studies in Income and Wealth*, NBER Conference on Research in Income and Wealth, 34, 1969, pp. 201–30.

Schwartzman, David, *The Decline of Service in Retail Trade: An Analysis of the Growth of Sales per Man-Hour, 1919–1963* (Pullman, WA: Washington State University Press, 1971).

Schwartzman, David, "Competition and Efficiency: Comment," *Journal of Political Economy*, Vol. 81, No. 3, May–June, 1973, pp. 756–64.

Schwartzman, D., *Innovation in the Pharmaceutical Industry* (Baltimore, MD: Johns Hopkins University Press, 1976).

Schweitzer, S.O., *Pharmaceutical Economics and Policy* (New York: Oxford University Press, 1997).

Shepherd, William G., *The Economics of Industrial Organization*, 4th edn (Upper Saddle River, NJ: Prentice Hall, 1997).

Shut, F.T. and P.A.G. Van Bergeijk, "International Price Discrimination: The Pharmaceutical Industry," *World Development*, Vol. 14, No. 9, 1986, pp. 1141–50.

Smith, Adam, *An Inquiry into the Nature and Causes of the Wealth of Nations*, gen. eds R.H. Campbell, and A.S. Skinner, textual ed. W.B. Todd (Oxford: Clarendon Press, 1976).

Solow, Robert M., "Technical Change and the Aggregate Production Function," *Review of Economics and Statistics*, Vol. 39, August, 1957, pp. 312–20.

Spencer, Barbara J. and James A. Brander, "International R&D and Industrial Strategy," *Review of Economic Studies*, Vol. 50, No. 4, October, 1983, pp. 707–22.

Spinanger, Dean, "Textile Beyond the MFA Phase-Out," Center for the Study of Globalization and Regionalization (CSGR), University of Warwick, Coventry, UK, Working Paper No. 13/98, July, 1998.

Staiger, R., and Wolak, "Measuring Industry-Specific Protection: Antidumping in the United States," *Brookings Papers: Microeconomics 1994* (Washington, DC: Brookings Institution Press), pp. 51–118.

Standard & Poor's "Industry Survey," July, 1995, M89.

Stigler, George J. "A Note on Price Discrimination in Steel," *American Economic Review*, Vol. 32, No.2, June, 1942, pp. 354–5.

Stigler, George J., *The Organization of Industry* (Chicago, IL: University of Chicago Press, 1968).

Stiglitz. Joseph E., "Dumping on Free Trade: The US Import Trade Laws," *Southern Economic Journal*, 1997, Vol. 64, No. 2, pp. 402–24.

Stock, James H. and Mark W. Watson, "Variable Trends in Economic Time Series," in R.F. Engle and C.W.J. Granger, eds, *Long-Run Economic Relationships: Readings in Cointegration* (Oxford: Oxford University Press, 1991), pp. 17–50.

Stolper, Wolfgang, and Paul A. Samuelson, "Protection and Real Wages," *Review of Economic Studies*, Vol. 9, No. 1, November, 1941, pp. 58–73.

Studenmund, A.H., *Using Econometrics: A Practical Guide*, 3rd edn (New York: Addison-Wesley, 1997).

Sturgeon, Timothy and Richard Florida, "Globalization, Deverticalization, and Employment in the Motor Vehicle Industry," in Martin Kenny and Richard Florida, eds, *Locating Global Advantage: Industry Dynamics in the International Economy* (Stanford University Press, 2004), pp. 52–81.

Szenberg, Michael, John W. Lombardi, and Eric Y. Lee, *Welfare Effects of Trade Restrictions: A Case Study of the US Footwear Industry*, with foreword by Robert E. Baldwin (New York: Academic Press, 1977).

Szenberg, Michael and Eric Y Lee, "The Structure of the American Book Publishing Industry," *Journal of Cultural Economics*, Vol. 18, 1994, pp. 313–22.

Szenberg, Michael "Disseminating Scholarly Output: The Case for Eliminating the Exclusivity of Journal Submissions," *American Journal of Economics and Sociology*, July, 1994, pp. 303–15.

Taggart, J., *The World Pharmaceutical Industry* (London: Routledge, 1993).

TEA-F-6 (1964), General Plywood.

TEA-F-10, Tariff Commission Pub. No. 23 (1970); TEA-W-15/18, Trade Commission Pub. 323 (1970), "Women's Shoe".

TEA-I-18, Tariff Commission Pub. No. 359 (1971), "Nonrubber Footwear".

Thomas, L.G., "Implicit Industrial Policy: The Triumph of Britain and the Failure of France in Global Pharmaceuticals," *Industrial and Corporate Change*, Vol. 3, No. 2, 1994, pp. 451–89.

Thomas, L.G., "Industrial Policy and International Competitiveness," in R.B. Helms, ed., *Competitive Strategies in the Pharmaceutical Industry* (Washington, DC: American Enterprice Institute) Press, 1996), pp. 107–29.

Thomas, R.L., *Modern Econometrics* (New York: Addison-Wesley, 1996).

Thompson, P. and D. Waldo, "Process versus Product Innovation: Do Consumption Data Contain Any Information?," *Southern Economic Journal*, Vol. 67 No. 1, 2000, pp. 155–70.

Tirole, J., *The Theory of Industrial Organization* (Cambridge, MA: The MIT Press, 1997).

Tornell, Aaron, "Rational Atrophy: The United States Steel Industry," (Washington DC: NBER Working Paper 6084, July, 1997).

Transmission Tower, Tariff Commission Pub. No. 298 (November 1969).

Trela, Irene and John Whalley, "Global Effects of Developed Country Trade Restrictions on Textiles and Apparel," *The Economic Journal*, Vol. 100, December, 1990, pp. 1190–1205.

United Nations, "United Nations Conference on Trade and Development: E-Commerce and Development Report," 2002. Source: http://www.unctad.org/ecommerce/.

United States International Trade Commission (ITC). "The Economic Effects of Significant US Import Restraints," June, 2002.

US Congress, Office of Technology Assessment, *Trade Adjustment Assistance: New Ideas for an Old Program-Special Report*, OTA-ITE-346 (Washington, DC: Government Printing Office, June, 1987).

USDC, *A Competitive Assessment of the US Pharmaceutical Industry* (Boulder, CO: Westview Press, 1986).

USITC, "Economy-Wide Modeling of the Economic Implications of a FTA with Mexico and a NAFTA with Canada and Mexico" (Washington, DC: United States International Trade Commission, May, 1992, Publication No. 2508).

USITC, "The Economic Effects of Significant US Import Restraints: Second Update" (Washington, DC: United States International Trade Commission, May, 1992, Publication No. 3201).

USITC, "Industry and Trade Summary: Apparel" (Washington, DC: International Trade Commission, January, 1995, Publication 2853).

USITC, "The Economic Effects of Significant US Import Restraints: First Biannual Update" (Washington, DC: United States International Trade Commission, December, 1995, Publication No. 2935).

USITC, "The Economic Effects of Significant US Import Restraints," Second Update 1999, Investigation No. 332–25, Publication 3201, May 1999.

USITC, "Operation of the Trade Agreements Program: The Year in Trade, 1998," (USITC Publication 3192, May, 1999).

USITC, "The Economic Effects of Significant US Import Restraints, Fourth Update 2004," June 2004, Investigation No. 332–25, Publication 3701.

Varian, Hal, "High-Technology Industries and Market Structure," in Federal Reserve Bank of Kansas City (FRB), *Economic Policy for the Information Economy* (Kansas City: The Federal Reserve Bank of Kansas City, 2001), pp. 65–102.

Weintraub, Sidney, "Potential for Hemispheric Regional Cooperation," in Sidney Weintraub, Alan M. Rugman, and Garvan Boyd, eds, *Free Trade in the Americas* (Northampton, MA: Edward Elgar, 2004).

Wright, Gavin, "The Origins of American Industrial Success, 1989–1940," *American Economic Review*, Vol. 80, No. 4, September, 1990, pp. 651–68.

Yang, Yongzheng, Will Martin and Koji Yanagishima, "Evaluating the Benefits of Abolishing the MFA in the Uruguay Round Package," in Thomas W. Hertel, ed., *Global Trade Analysis: Modeling and Application* (New York: Cambridge University Press, 1997).

Index